John …

Thanks for your interest.

Jean Haubrich Cosgrove
'94

COPING W I T H

Teen
Gambling

by Jane Haubrich-Casperson
with Doug Van Nispen

THE ROSEN PUBLISHING GROUP, INC./NEW YORK

Published in 1993 by The Rosen Publishing Group, Inc.
29 East 21st Street, New York, NY 10010

First Edition

Library of Congress Cataloging-in-Publication Data

Haubrich-Casperson, Jane.
    Coping with teen gambling/by Jane Haubrich-Casperson, with Doug Van Nispen.—1st ed.
        p.   cm.
    Includes bibliographical references and index.
    Summary: Discusses the phenomenon of compulsive gambling among teenagers, how to recognize the signs of addiction, and steps that can be taken to deal with this problem.
    ISBN 0-8239-1512-3
    1. Compulsive gambling—United States—Juvenile literature.
    2. Obsessive-compulsive disorder in adolescence—United States—Juvenile literature.   3. Compulsive gamblers—Family relationships—Juvenile literature.   [1. Gambling.   2. Obsessive-compulsive disorder.]   I. Van Nispen, Doug.   II. Title.
    HV6715.H38   1993
    362.2'5—dc20   92-41549
                                                                          CIP
                                                                          AC

ABOUT THE AUTHORS ⬦

Jane Haubrich-Casperson is a Nationally Certified Gambling Counselor and a member of the National Council on Problem Gambling. Armed with a degree in Youth Ministry, a background in addiction training, and six years as a hotline volunteer for troubled teens, she developed the first statewide hotline in Minnesota for compulsive gamblers. The hotline was jointly sponsored by the Minnesota Department of Human Services and the Minnesota Council on Compulsive Gambling.

While serving as the Hotline Coordinator, Ms. Haubrich-Casperson came in contact daily with those affected by the destructive forces of compulsive gambling. She became convinced of the need for public education and prevention of compulsive gambling behavior, and the seeds were planted for a book about young people's gambling.

Presently, Jane, whose zest for life in midlife rivals that of her young readers, finds time to care for her family, write poetry, act in community theater, and speak to teens and their parents about the dangers of compulsive gambling.

Doug Van Nispen is a Nationally Certified Gambling Counselor and a recovering compulsive gambler. Since 1980, he has worked in the chemical dependency unit at Miller Dwan Medical Center, Duluth, Minnesota. Along with his duties as a Gambling counselor, Doug spent many hours meeting with kids and recording their stories about their involvement with gambling addiction.

Doug has also worked with the Minnesota Council on Compulsive Gambling as a specialist in adolescent gambling prevention. He has been featured on ABC's "Good Morning America" and the NBC Evening News with Tom Brokaw for his work with adolescents. When not tending his prize huskies or running a marathon, he continues to spread the word about the dangers of compulsive gambling to teens, educators, and parents.

Contents

Foreword

I find particular pleasure in welcoming readers to this carefully compiled, accurately referenced, easy to read, and extremely practical book. The work clearly reflects the authors' deep understanding and expertise derived from their face-to-face experiences in counseling youthful pathological gamblers.

The release of *Coping with Teen Gambling* is particularly timely. It comes on the heels of a series of recent research reports that for the first time have documented the extent, age at onset, varied types of wagering done, and problems associated with teenage gambling in America. These studies, completed during the period 1985–1990, have involved over 3,700 ninth- to twelfth-grade students from seventeen high schools in California, Minnesota, Virginia, New Jersey, and Connecticut. Results suggest that throughout the forty-eight states that currently legalize some form of gambling, one can expect to find about half of their high school age youth had gambled for money in the past twelve months, and that one in ten has serious gambling-related problems. Indeed, the same studies indicate that the prevalence of compulsive/pathological gambling among that teenage sample (4–6 percent) is over three times that reported for adults (1.4 percent) in a recent study sponsored by the National Institute for Mental Health.

It is difficult to understand how a phenomenon so pervasive, openly practiced, and patently illegal as juvenile gambling could continue in virtually every jurisdiction in the United States without drawing the attention of the media, much less the authorities. Even more confounding is the likelihood, stemming from the studies noted above, that millions of legally underage youth could be buying lottery tickets at stores in their own neighborhoods from tens of thousands of state-sanctioned lottery vendors, placing bets at scores of state-licensed horse and dog tracks, playing at hundreds of municipally registered bingo games, and (to a lesser extent) wagering at casinos, commercial card parlors, jai alai games, and legalized off-track betting emporia without being challenged ("carded") and unceremoniously ejected.

The apparent unwillingness of adults in our society to acknowledge potential hazards in the extensive gambling behaviors of adolescents may arise from their belief that legal sanctions will discourage any "really serious" gambling among those under eighteen years of age—so, not to worry. Another reason may be the hesitancy of adult society to face up to its own role in fostering childhood and teenage gambling, since the overwhelming majority of young people who gamble were introduced to the diversion by their parents or older relatives. Over a third of the students involved in the studies noted above reported that they had first gambled for money before their eleventh birthday, and over 80 percent said they had done so before they were fifteen years of age.

The data accumulated since the mid-1980s leads me to conclude (a) that for some years past, millions of teenagers have been placing bets on whatever social, legally sanctioned, and illegal games have been accessible to them, (b) that the extent of teenage gambling has been increasing steadily over recent years, and (c) that for a particularly vulnerable minority of teenagers, gambling can pose a serious threat to present and future well-being. It is for those reasons that I believe this book could not have appeared at a better time.

To my knowledge, this is the first book about problem gambling that addresses teenagers directly in a non-patronizing manner and speaks in terms they can identify with and apply to their own lives. It offers them the opportunity to assess themselves privately and objectively (by checklist) for early signs of problems in their own gambling activities. It even provides helpful suggestions about how to deal effectively, yet in a caring way, with peers who have gambling-related problems.

This book holds answers for parents who ask, "How can I know if my child is in trouble with gambling—and where can I go for help?" They also may gain some insight into how their attempts to reduce their own stress levels through escape into gambling and other excessive behaviors may impact on their children.

The finding that one in ten high school age students has reported serious gambling-related problems, coupled with increasing numbers of media accounts about students "making book" on sports betting in junior high and senior high school corridors should put teachers, counselors, and school administrators on notice that gambling is a fact of life in their institutions. Besides learning much from this book, educators will find its content readily adaptable for inclusion in ongoing school-based programs about tobacco, alcohol, drugs, and overeating, since all these potentially addictive substances and activities are fellow travelers among adolescents.

Those of us in the helping professions are deeply indebted to these authors for creating a treatise that can serve so many so well. *Coping with Teen Gambling* provides a viable means for effectively intercepting adolescents early on the road to greater troubles, and thereby may have a significant influence on reducing the ranks of tomorrow's pathological gamblers.

Durand F. Jacobs, Ph.D., ABPP
First Vice President,
National Council on Problem Gambling

Recipient of the Herman Goldman Foundation Award

Acknowledgments

My special appreciation to Dean, my husband, for his encouragement, and my children, Kelly, Hans, and Tim, whose enthusiasm for life continually recharges my own;

Dr. Durand F. Jacobs, a truly wise and gentle man, and Dr. Henry Lesieur, for their supportive comments and suggestions;

The National Council on Problem Gambling, especially Mary with her eager response to numerous requests for reprints and sources;

The New Jersey, Florida, and Nevada Councils, affiliates of the NCPG, and Tabor, of the Canadian Council, who provided leads and info;

Olivia, a young woman who possesses wisdom beyond her years, and Judi, for their willingness to share their stories so that others may have the courage to hope for a better day;

Molly, whose support and belief in the process has been unwavering, and Penny, for her reflections and insights on life;

Joanna Franklin, Sergeant Butch Wegman, Michael and Dennis of the Intervention Institute, Arnie Wexler, Dr. Lynn Rambeck, Dr. Ken Winters, Jeannie LeTourneau, Jim Sherman, and Jamie—all willing to share their precious time;

The Rosen Publishing Group for believing in kids and giving me this opportunity.

My thanks also to Doug and the many GA members

who embody the power of a 12-Step program and the tenacity of the human spirit to find serenity.

Finally, thank you to all the young people who bravely shared their life stories so that others may learn from their examples. Most of their names have been changed to protect those who wish to remain anonymous.

Jane Haubrich-Casperson

"Doug's Story" is dedicated to Tony Oliva. "I started as your fan, you grew to be my hero, and now I call you friend." Tony, you will always be in my heart's Hall of Fame!

Dave Griffith, thanks for all your help and support but most of all for being a friend.

Doug Van Nispen

Introduction

Okay, here's a trick question for you: What is the fastest-growing addictive behavior in America today? A) smoking, B) drinking, C) drugs, D) none of the above. If you answered "none of the above" you're on the right track so far. Now, would you be able to guess the correct answer if you knew that the addiction of the '90s does not involve shooting anything into your veins, does not require you to place anything in your mouth to inhale, and does not consist of drinking or swallowing a substance? Ready to give up?

The answer is GAMBLING!

Gambling? You didn't know gambling could be an addictive behavior? Well, it can be. Just how attractive this potentially addictive activity has become is demonstrated by the ever-increasing numbers of young people who are experimenting with various types of gambling behaviors and devices.

So what is behind the explosion of gambling by teens, and why haven't you heard any preventive or educational messages regarding its potential danger?

One reason is that, like you, most adults are not aware that gambling can be addictive. Additionally, many adults are not conscious of the large amount of gambling, wagering, and betting that kids are doing. If parents do have an idea that their kids are buying lottery tickets, betting on sports teams, or playing cards and counting points for money, they dismiss the activities as harmless fun.

"What's the big deal?" some parents may be thinking. "At least, they're not getting loaded, stoned, or messing up their lungs!"

That might be true. But how concerned would your parents be if you were engaged in an activity that could cause depression so severe that you would even think about committing suicide? Would they be concerned if you were involved in something that could cause you to lose all your hard-earned money—and theirs too?

What about you? Would you be worried if you lost your friends, your reputation, and an opportunity to attend the school or college of your choice? Would you be alarmed if you owed money to so many of your friends that you began stealing from family members or selling your cherished CD player, athletic shoes, or leather team jacket?

When gambling takes over your life, many of the people and possessions that are important to you are left behind and pushed aside. A person who is addicted to gambling cares about only one thing—finding enough money, through any means possible, to keep on gambling.

It's curious that an activity like gambling has become so popular among young people, and that some adults are so concerned for those who are beginning to gamble. To understand this phenomenon, let's look at the history of gambling and how it evolved in our country to the present day.

Gambling is not new, although the wide variety of opportunities may make it seem so. Since ancient times, people have played games of chance. Excavations at ancient cities of Babylonia and the Far East have revealed symmetrical bones and stones that were very likely used in betting and predictions. Even the Bible mentions casting or drawing lots.

Many European countries have operated some form of lottery for centuries. Dice-playing among foot soldiers as well as among kings and noblemen is noted during the Middle Ages.

The development of our own country's infrastructure often relied upon lotteries to provide funding. In 1612 a lottery helped the settlers finance the first colony. George Washington used a lottery to raise funds for a road to lead pioneers westward. And in 1776 the Revolutionary Army received support through a lottery established by the Continental Congress. Lotteries were even used to fund such prestigious colleges as Harvard, Yale, and Princeton.

As gambling on lotteries became widespread, so did abuses connected with them. After all, cheating is not new to humankind either!

In the late 1800s a particularly corrupt lottery, the Louisiana Lottery, pushed the public's tolerance of legalized gambling to its limit. Soon every state as well as the federal government outlawed lotteries and most gambling of all types.

But because people seem to love to gamble, the legal prohibitions began to soften by the mid-1900s. Gradually gambling was legalized in certain areas, such as Las Vegas and Atlantic City.

Some state governments allowed private organizations, including churches and community clubs, to hold bingo games and raffles for charitable purposes. The thinking seemed to be that as long as the money raised went for some beneficial cause, certain types of gambling could be allowed.

It was not until the mid-1960s that state governments got into the gambling business in a big way. Then too, however, the proceeds were to benefit society. New Hampshire established the first state-operated lottery; New York followed with a monthly lottery, with the proceeds earmarked for education. Massachusetts and New Jersey quickly followed, as did California and Florida. State governments were discovering that gambling in the form of lotteries could make big money for much-needed programs.

To date, more than thirty-two states have joined the rush to fund public enterprises with money from government-run gambling. State governments have touted lotteries as a voluntary and painless way to raise money without raising taxes in tight economic times. These lotteries, instant scratch-off tickets, daily Pick-3s, and Power Ball tickets are big business, raising billions of dollars each year.

Another explosion of gambling opportunities was the development of gaming casinos on Indian reservations. Because of a U.S. Supreme Court ruling in 1987 and passage of the Indian Gaming Regulatory Act in 1988, Indian communities constructed elaborate casinos on tribal land. With Las Vegas-style games of blackjack, video slots, poker, keno, and bingo, people who had never set foot in a casino before began to gamble.

One Indian casino in a rural Minnesota town of 200 boasts that it is the largest casino between the East Coast and Las Vegas. The Tribal Councils, like state governments, see the tremendous economic advantage provided by the millions of dollars earned from these gambling emporiums. Gambling offers the Native American people a way out of poverty and a reduction in their dependence on federal funds.

Many positive results have come from the billions of dollars generated by state-run lotteries, Indian gaming casinos, and charitable gambling games. Proceeds have been used for economic development, education, wildlife preservation, and youth programs. Jobs have been created in areas where the unemployment previously was as high as 25 percent.

What has been ignored, however, in this rush to capitalize on the public's love of gambling, is the addictive quality of gambling and the consequences of teenage compulsive gambling. With more and more opportunities to gamble bombarding kids through newspapers, radio, and television, more and more adolescents are gambling for the first time. Of those who continue to gamble, between 2 and 6 percent have become addicted and fit the definition of pathological or compulsive gambler.

With the intense marketing efforts of casinos and multimillion-dollar promotions of lotteries, a message is being sent to young people like yourself that to succeed in life, all you need to do is win the big jackpot. Although it is illegal in all states to gamble if you are under eighteen (and in many states if you are under twenty-one), plenty of evidence suggests that teens see gambling as an alternative to hard work and education.

Upon questioning one Midwestern sophomore class recently, several of the students expressed the sincere belief that they were going to win the million-dollar state lottery. For that reason, they concluded, there really was no need to study any longer. The attitude of these students, who were already buying lottery tickets and pulling tabs, was one of genuine conviction. By placing a few dollars on the numbers or scratching a few tickets, they believed, they could forget the hassles of life and the normal routes to success. To these kids, winning means no work, no sweat, no grief.

But wait a second. Isn't that the same lie conveyed

by other potentially addicting substances? Take a drink, mellow out, and forget that your boyfriend just dumped you. Snort a line of coke, start flying high, and become brighter and sexier than anyone else in the room. Keep shaking those dice, slamming down those cards, pulling those tabs, scratching those tickets, and you'll be a millionaire. Right? WRONG!

There is a downside to gambling that you need to know. Very few people are winners. Casinos and lotteries are in business to make money, not to give it away. In 1991, *USA TODAY* reported that the gambling industry (both legal and illegal) showed gross receipts of close to $100 billion dollars. One year later, estimates of money spent on gambling by the American public range close to $300 billion, an increase of over three hundred percent.

To have billions of dollars in profits, there must be billions of losers. It is estimated that as much as 7.5 percent of gamblers who are losing their money by betting are not just financially strapped.[1] These losers have given up friends, families, possessions—and some have even lost their lives.

You and your friends have to cope with gambling as no generation before you has. Whether or not your parents know anything about gambling; even if the lotteries and casinos are not willing to look at the growing numbers of young people who are destroying their lives by gambling; and despite the fact that all your friends seem to be gambling, you need to be informed so that you can make a reasoned decision whether or not this is something in which you choose to be involved.

Just as with choices about drugs, smoking, and drinking, you need to know the negative consequences that can result when you choose to place that first bet. That's what this book is about.

CHAPTER 1

Doug's Story

I work in a large medical center. My job is doing group work with kids who have entered the chemical dependency treatment program—kids who are addicted to drugs or alcohol.

Upon entering the program, some of these kids look really beaten and broken in spirit. Some are real cocky, not yet ready to admit that they have messed up. But by the time they enter their first group encounter with their peers, the reality of their situation has started to sink in. Their lives are out of control, and they need help.

I usually ask these kids how many of them thought they would end up in a treatment program when they took their first drink. Of course, no hands go up. Who could possibly believe, while gulping down their first beer, that they might become addicted to alcohol?

What you need to know about gambling is that it is similar to use of alcohol. For many people, enjoying a drink or two is a harmless way to blow off steam, release stress. Gambling, for most people, is a harmless form of entertainment. Place a few bets, scratch a few tickets, or play some video slots for fun, and walk away. No harm done.

Nobody takes a first drink expecting to get hooked on alcohol. Likewise, nobody scratches the first lottery ticket expecting to become a compulsive gambler. But some kids develop problems with excessive drinking; others develop problems with excessive (compulsive) gambling. The dilemma is this: No one knows who will become addicted and who won't.

What is known about both addictions is that each has an ever-increasing level of involvement that creates a downward spiral. No one escapes the swirling motion once the addiction takes over except by seeking help through treatment and counseling. The only option that lies at the bottom of the spiral is death: either through accident or suicide.

When I first started to gamble, I never thought I could end up losing most of the things that were precious in my life. I didn't think I would become a liar and a cheat either, but I did. I'm certainly not proud of the way I messed up with compulsive gambling, but I hope that by reading my story you will be able to understand this addiction and the consequences that can follow.

I placed my first bet when I was eleven. It was winter where I lived, and winter meant snow. Lots of snow.

My friends and I made spending money by shoveling snow. We'd carry our shovels around the neighborhood, asking if we could clear the walks for pay. Since Mother Nature piled sidewalks waist deep in the white stuff that winter, we made good money.

After finishing work for the day, all the guys headed over to Steve's house to warm up. Steve's father was not employed at the time, so he was usually at home when we arrived. It was Steve's Dad who taught all of us to play poker.

Playing poker with the guys. What a great way to pass the hours during the darkest part of the afternoon. Here I was with the guys, having fun and feeling like I belonged. That was really important to a shy person like myself.

Poker was easy to learn, and Steve's Dad, who always seemed to have a drink in his hand, showed us how to keep score with matchsticks. We enjoyed playing and keeping track of points with the matches, until someone suggested that we use our shoveling money to bet on the hands and make the game more exciting.

Now we were "really" playing poker just like the men in the Western movies. The cards were dealt, we'd place our bets, and play out our hands. Then it was "read 'em and weep" time to see who would capture the pot of money.

What started as a harmless game to pass the time quickly began to be taken seriously. Some of us were losing our hard-earned money. It was the only extra money several of us had, since none of our families were well off.

I wasn't the worst poker player in the group, but I began to lose often. I watched my nickels, dimes, and pretty soon my quarters disappear. Though the guys teased me a lot and said I should call it quits, I was determined that wouldn't happen. I wasn't a quitter.

Besides, hanging out with these guys, being accepted as one of them, was really important to me. It was fun to gamble, and I was getting attention from my peers. That was something I desperately needed, because I sure wasn't getting any positive strokes at home.

My family were having problems, and at that time of

my life I was very needy and vulnerable. See, my mom drank a lot. I didn't understand it then, but now I know she was an alcoholic.

You've heard the saying, there's no place like home? At my house, in a twisted way, that was certainly true. In fact, the less time I spent there, the better. Mom was always drunk, or trying to get more booze so she could get drunk. Dad was gone a lot because he worked two jobs. When he finally came home, the fights would start between them. And when Dad was worn out from yelling at Mom for getting drunk, he'd start yelling at me for not keeping the bottles away from her.

It's easy to see why a kid would go to his friend's house every day and play cards for money rather than go home and listen to the screaming. Even though I was losing all my money, there was no way I could be enticed to stay away from the warm companionship at the poker table only to return to a home in constant chaos.

After I had lost all my money, I became desperate to stay in the game. "I can't quit," I thought. "If I just hang in a little longer, my luck's bound to change."

I began to bet my record albums (oh, what I wouldn't give to have some of those original Rolling Stones and Beatles albums now). When those were gone, I bet my Daisy BB gun. I lost that too.

It seemed that just when I was beginning to feel good about myself, things started to go wrong. The good feelings I sought were connected to gambling. In the process of trying to be a winner, I was becoming a loser.

The poker games finally came to an end when the parents of one of the guys saw him bringing home the loot I had lost. They called my folks, and the shouting at home really accelerated.

My parents forbade me to go to Steve's house or ever to gamble again, and since there was enough yelling at our house normally, I figured I had learned my lesson. Besides, I really wanted to be a good kid. My fear was that by gambling on cards I had done something bad, and that meant I was a bad person. I was finished with gambling for a while.

But life at home continued to get worse. Unfortunately, coping skills to handle stress were not taught in school at the time. I soon turned to another negative way to cope with the tension of living in a troubled family. I ate—a lot.

Since I was tall for my age, eating to excess caused me to be huge physically. It became pretty hard to hide in a crowd at school because I weighed 235 pounds and was almost six feet tall. I became "Funny Doug," the one with the sense of humor, the big, fat guy.

At home, however, I was still the one who was blamed for most everything that went wrong. Dad had appointed me Mom's protector. This designation made me the one who was supposed to keep her away from liquor. But Mom, like any addicted person, was very sneaky. If she had nothing to drink in the house, she would call a liquor store and have a cab deliver the booze to the house.

When Dad would find out about the latest delivery, I would be blamed.

I wished I could just disappear, become invisible. Trying to hide inside my weight, to avoid the shaming and blaming, wasn't working. So I took to hanging out in the cellar.

That cellar became my first safe hiding place. I took my transistor radio down in that damp, dark hole and listened to baseball. The Minnesota Twins were my favorite team, and sitting there alone, eating my DingDong cakes, I'd dream of being a big-league baseball player like my idol, Tony Oliva.

Tony was an outfielder, Rookie of the Year in 1964. Boy, how I wanted to be like him, running fast, winning batting championships. If you ever wished you could be Kirby Puckett or Michael Jordan, you'll understand how much I worshiped Tony Oliva.

The Twins and Tony pulled me through a terrible summer when I became an adolescent. As autumn arrived, the warring between Mom and Dad was just getting worse, so I decided to live with my Grandma Petra. No formal arrangement was made between Grandma and my parents. I just began staying at her house more and more until finally I didn't go home anymore. I was the incredible disappearing kid, and nobody seemed to notice.

Grandma's house became my second safe refuge. She wasn't home very often herself, since she worked long hours at a bakery. But I didn't mind. It was a perfect setup for a troubled fat kid. All the pastries I could devour were waiting for me every time I came home. Even though I was frequently alone, at least I wasn't faced with the bickering I hated so much at my parents' house.

During my junior year in high school, I began to notice girls. I also began to notice that they weren't noticing me—except for how funny and fat I was. Slowly, I realized how different I was from most of the guys. I was hiding within my big body, and I began to feel lousy. I really thought I was a total zero.

It occurred to me that maybe I could be somebody if I lost weight. Then the other kids would like me. Runners are skinny, I observed. I could take up running and make the wall of fat I was hiding behind vanish.

There was only one problem: I was so ashamed of my

body that I couldn't bring myself to run during the daylight hours. I thought my friends would jeer when they saw me exercising and jogging. So I began running in the dark, at night. Grandma, exhausted at the end of a day, didn't notice me sneaking out at midnight to begin my run.

At first, I couldn't run a block without getting winded. But gradually I built up my endurance and ran longer and longer distances. I discovered that running made me feel good, so I wanted to do more of it.

That summer, I lost forty pounds in two months. Returning to school in the fall, I got noticed. In fact, I had lost so much weight so fast that my classmates wondered if I had developed cancer.

No longer was I the funny, fat kid. I was the lean, mean running machine. I became obsessed with running. If I didn't run five miles every day, I didn't feel good. If I had to work after school until ten o'clock, I couldn't go to sleep until I had run my miles for the day.

I joined a Legion baseball team and rekindled my dreams of becoming a major-league player. My life, for all its ups and downs, seemed to be going pretty well. I finished high school, got a job in construction, and got married. Then my first accident happened.

While working on a large construction job, I fell and chipped a bone in my right ankle. Hospitalized for several days, all I could dwell on was how much I missed my running. I also was facing the possibility of being unable to work for several months.

The day after I was released from the hospital, with a cast on my leg, my second accident occurred. I was riding in an old pick-up truck with some buddies from work; we were just out cruising to have some fun. Though none of us were drunk, the driver had been drinking during the afternoon. I'm not certain how the accident happened, but we hit a cement pillar at high speed, and I went through the windshield.

I shattered my left wrist, smashed my face, and tore my hip from its socket. The gashes on my face required over 100 stitches to repair, and I needed plastic surgery. Pieces of my pelvic bone were used to rebuild my wrist during the next nine months.

During this time, I became increasingly disheartened with my marriage. The relationship, which had never been truly happy, deteriorated even more. Shortly after the accident, my wife and I were divorced.

This accident ended all chances of returning to construction work or any kind of heavy labor. It certainly ended my dreams of becoming a major-league ball player. The old feelings of emptiness and abandonment were returning.

I was a loser again, just as I had been ever since junior high. If anyone needed proof, I had only to cite my recent losses as evidence: my marriage, my job, my health and physical abilities, my self-esteem. I had to face it, I was a mess.

After months in the hospital, I was released to begin a long recovery period. The only job I could find that I could handle physically was tending bar. So I poured the drinks for customers and watched them enjoy their favorite pastime—gambling.

In this particular bar, gambling was not done on the sly; it was open. In fact, as a bartender, I handed out the bookie's betting sheets to the customers. Gambling was a customary activity among my coworkers: They gambled on sports and placed bets with the bookie while on the job.

Everyone seemed to be having a great time watching

the football games, placing bets, and collecting the winnings when their team was successful. When someone hit big, congratulations were given all around.

I began thinking I was at least as smart as those people who were betting and winning. I had played and listened to enough sports in my life to know winning teams when I saw them. Besides, with my broken body, this was about as close to major league sports as I was ever going to get. So why not bet a few bucks, win some money, and gather a few of those back slaps and "way-to-go's" for myself?

I studied the teams, placed a couple of small bets, and won. And I won, AND I WON! What a great way to get attention. I was Doug, the winner, not Doug, the loser. This is the first phase of compulsive gambling, called the winning phase.

I didn't realize it at the time, but I had just developed the perfect formula for failure. Once again I was looking outside of myself to make myself feel good. With all the losses I had experienced, I was very vulnerable to losing control of my life to some addictive behavior. It could have been alcohol, it could have been drugs, but I chose gambling.

Why? Because I had already learned at the age of eleven that I felt good when I was in the action. Gambling was familiar, and I recalled how happy I had felt being one of the guys sitting around the poker table. At a time when I felt a huge empty cavity inside myself, I believed I could fill it by gambling. It had worked once for me; maybe it would work again.

There's a tricky thing about addictive behavior, however. It causes the addicted person not to see the truth of what is going on in his life. This lie, this denial of reality, caused me not to look at the negative consequences of the first time I tried gambling.

Betting on football, playing the boards was thrilling! I was older and smarter now than that wimpy eleven-year-old who lost his snow-shoveling money and his prized possessions.

I started out betting one game at a time, then went to two games and then five. Betting and winning $20 felt good. But after a while, $20 was no big thrill, so I bet $30. Then, when I'd win $50 back, I couldn't see why I should bet only small amounts again. I was hooked.

Compulsive gambling is like alcoholism or drug addiction. Once you start using and increasing your drug of choice, you don't go backward and decrease it. An addict thinks, if it took a certain amount to get high before, a little more this time might bring a better high. That is deluded thinking.

As the gambling addiction started taking over my life, I needed ever-increasing bets, and wins, to feel better about myself. The highs needed to be higher. Before long, I was betting $200 to $500 per night.

Gamblers have a sense that they are different and special when they are winning, and that's how I began to feel. All my life I had been told I was dumb, but now I knew I was smart because I was picking the winners. And everybody loves a winner.

Customers would cheer the games I had bet while they watched the big-screen television in the bar. Heck, they were cheering for me, asking me for advice about how to place their bets next time. When I won, I bought a round of drinks. When I lost, well, that was blamed on bad luck. I justified the losses by saying that my system of picking the teams just needed refining.

By betting so heavily on more and more games, in truth, I was lowering my odds. Did this stop me from throwing my money away on gambling? No way. I even added to the amount I was spending on gambling by buying information for each game.

For $500 a month, I bought the services of a man from New York who sold information about team statistics, player injuries, and even the weather forecasts for the game sites. Using his information, I did win. In fact, I had a big win in December. I was hot; my service was hot. I thought the guy was magical, and I wanted to stick with him at all costs. There was only one problem: Neither my paycheck nor my winnings covered all the money I was spending on gambling.

In succession, I had several losses that set me back hundreds of dollars. I began to bet even more heavily, trying to win back what I had lost. If I was down $500 one night, I would bet a thousand dollars trying to win back part of what I had lost. A person who does not gamble compulsively would stop after several large losses. But a compulsive gambler thinks that because he has lost several nights in a row, it's his turn to hit. I believed that, and no way would I quit now.

I began to run out of the insurance money from my accidents, and I tapped my savings. My house was paid for, but I took out another loan on it to cover the mounting debts to my bookie.

As a sports bettor, I didn't have to pay the bookie up front. If I owed him $3,600 and didn't have a penny to pay him, I figured I might as well try to get myself out by betting more. If I couldn't come up with money I already owed, it didn't matter to me if I bet several thousand more that I didn't have. I just kept trying to win it back. That is called chasing losses.

I bet on everything: football, basketball, hockey. I worried all day about where I would get money to gamble on the games, and I was in a state of panic until I had the bets placed. I agonized at night, losing sleep thinking about how I would bet the next day to make up my losses. I neglected my friends and my family. I told Mom I wouldn't come to a holiday family dinner unless I could have the game on TV. I'd sneak into the bathroom to listen on the radio if I wasn't near a TV. My health was suffering too. I skipped meals and filled up on junk food while I nervously watched the games I had bet.

Occasionally I stopped gambling for a while, but not by choice. I owed my bookie so much that he wouldn't take any more bets until I paid up. At these times I tried to get things back in balance—until it was okay in my mind to start placing small bets again.

My behavior, when I look back, was like that of the alcoholic who tries to stop drinking for a while. An alcoholic thinks he can handle his drinking. He tries to prove it by drinking only a small amount or even by stopping completely for a while. But it never works, because the problem isn't how much he is drinking; the problem is that he is addicted to alcohol.

I wouldn't admit that I was a compulsive gambler, and I kept trying to prove I wasn't every time I stopped gambling. I stopped as many as five times. I even changed jobs, leaving the bar business and eventually becoming a unit assistant in a chemical dependency center. I couldn't have an addiction problem, I told myself, if I was working on a CD unit in a hospital. I certainly wasn't as out of control as the alcoholics and drug addicts I was seeing.

But I was. Though I was physically at work, my mind, my thoughts, and my actions were on betting. When I came to work owing $1,500 to my bookie, my mind was not on how I could help the patients I was assigned.

All I needed was a phone to place bets, and that I had

at my job. I listened to a radio in the back room on my floor, unconcerned about those I was supposed to assist. After all, I had more money riding on a game than I would make in three months on the job.

It didn't take coworkers, or patients, long to figure out that I was a sports bettor. I told them I bet $20 on games, when in reality I had twenty times that much riding. When I was winning, I let everyone know. When I lost, I never told anybody.

That's why compulsive gambling is called the hidden illness. I didn't stumble when I walked, and my breath didn't smell of alcohol like the patients I worked with. But I was out of control now, and I carried my sickness into a new marriage.

I thought I was being totally honest with Jeanne by telling her that I liked to gamble occasionally. I insisted on keeping separate checking accounts so I could handle a few bills left over from past gambling debts.

Jeanne had no idea to what extent I gambled, however, nor did she realize that I wanted separate accounts so I could have the freedom to keep my addiction going. I took out personal loans using my car as collateral, then used the money to gamble, and Jeanne never knew.

I deceived my banker, too, telling him that the loan was to repair a roof. Over two years I borrowed enough money to put three new roofs on my house and two transmissions in my car. All a fraud.

I was leading a secret life, and it was killing me. My nerves were shot trying to juggle the mounting debts, and my stomach was in knots. I would run to the mailbox before Jeanne got home and tear up the overdue bills and the loan company notices. I'd try to cover up the calls from my bookie. And, late at night, I'd leave our bed because I couldn't sleep.

I was sick enough to believe, like the addicts I worked with, that I could control everything all the time. I was bound to slip up somewhere with all the details I was handling. Yet I couldn't think about my life without gambling. I was in the desperation phase of compulsive gambling and didn't even know it. Gambling had become a full-time obsession.

The football season was starting again. Secretly, I started to place a few bets on games, betting over $2,000 on weekdays and up to $3,000 on weekends. I was well over $30,000 in debt, and I tried to extend loans I already had. I devised a scheme to commit a crime: a way to get gambling money illegally—something I had never dreamed I was capable of doing.

The continual tension and pressure were making me ill both physically and mentally, and my temper was taking a toll on our marriage. One night, during another fight about lack of money, Jeanne threatened to leave me. Because I didn't want to lose my wife, I broke down and told her about all the gambling I was doing. I knew I needed help, but I was ashamed to talk to any of the counselors at work. So I tried to stay straight on my own. I promised to stop and did for a short while.

Slowly, I set up a plan to pay off my debts and began to work with Jeanne in seeking help for my gambling. Then the beginning of the end came for me. Grandma Petra died.

Grandma was the only person I felt had loved me unconditionally. She had been my solid foundation when my world was crumbling. Now she was gone. I felt abandoned and empty once again. That black pit inside me was opening wider and wider, and I couldn't seem to fill it. I knew only one way to escape the pain—gambling.

I went to the bank and took $1,500 out of a joint savings

account Jeanne and I had started when I first promised to stop gambling. I knew I couldn't hide what I had done from Jeanne, but I needed to gamble. So I lied and told her I was going to buy a new car. Then I called the bookie and placed a sucker bet, a bet I knew I was going to lose. I had never gambled on any team knowing that I was going to lose, but this time was different. I had had a chance to know what life was like without gambling, and I didn't want to go back to the craziness. I didn't want to lose any more, and it wasn't just money I didn't want to lose. That bet was my cry for help.

I called David, a counselor I had worked with on the chemical dependency unit, and explained to him what I had done. David helped me understand how my compulsive gambling was an addiction just like alcohol for the patients I worked with. I learned about a group called Gamblers Anonymous (GA), where I could find the help and support I needed to stop gambling. He urged me to attend.

Even though I was afraid, I did go to a GA meeting. There I found a warm welcome from people who had compulsively gambled just like me. But there was one difference between myself and those people: They had found a way to live without the insanity of a gambling addiction. I was ready to do that too.

I have stayed straight for three years through the help of my friends and GA. Because of my addiction to gambling, I had to sell my house and my car and borrow against my insurance to reduce the huge debt I had accumulated. Three years later, I'm still working to pay off loans made while I gambled out of control.

I can sometimes laugh now when I think how my addiction started with a few matchsticks and a nickel bet. I understand that I spent my whole life looking outside myself for peace and self-worth, when in reality I was capable of finding it within myself.

I know, when it comes to gambling, I have a choice whether or not I will do it. And that's what you need to know too.

CHAPTER ◇ 2

A Nation of
Gamblers

People who gamble to excess with seemingly total disregard for their own well-being or their family's economic and emotional health were not always considered to have an addiction. Until quite recently, anyone who gambled to such levels as to lose home, job, or loved ones was considered immoral, or at least to have some sort of personal weakness.

This view of the compulsive gambler as being of less than good moral character is similar to that held toward alcoholics about fifty years ago. Thanks to the early efforts of Bill W., who help to found Alcoholics Anonymous, and the pioneers in the field of alcoholism and chemical dependency treatment, no longer is addiction to alcohol or chemicals seen as a sign of moral depravity.

Beliefs are changing in much the same way about those with a gambling problem. The first formal attempt to establish another theory about compulsive gambling came from a group called Gamblers Anonymous, who first met in 1957. Using a program for recovery similar to the Alcoholics Anonymous 12-Step program, recognition of compulsive gambling as an illness was initiated. Also, professionals whose work involved treating addictive behaviors began to see similarities between the consequences of excessive gambling and other addictions.

Since those early steps toward acknowledging the serious consequences of problem gambling, America seems to have undergone a gambling boom. In 1974 the Commission on the Review of the National Policy Toward Gambling undertook a national survey of gambling behavior.[2] At that time, 61 percent of adults in the United States gambled. Through more recent surveys conducted by a widely divergent group of researchers (including the gaming industry itself), it is now estimated that 80 to 90 percent of the adult population engages in regular gambling of some type.

With increased legalization of gambling, and the intense marketing efforts to encourage participation, it could be expected that more people would gamble. Expansion of opportunities could also be correlated to an increase in the number of persons addicted to gambling. In fact, a report released in 1976 by the same commission noted a direct relation between the broadening of legalized gambling and an increase in compulsive gambling:

"Legalization of gambling increases public exposure to more types of gambling, reduces negative attitudes toward the other [illegal] types of gambling and encourages wider participation . . . Survey findings also indicate that the widespread availability of legal gambling causes an increase in the incidence of compulsive gambling . . ."

Well, the number of gamblers, and members of their families, seeking help for gambling problems did increase. Consequently, by the late 1970s and early '80s, no longer could the army of people seeking relief from their entanglement be easily dismissed as morally corrupt or weak-willed. Psychotherapists, researchers, and physicians, among them Dr. Robert Custer, Durand Jacobs, Ph.D., Valerie C. Lorenz, Ph.D., Dr. Richard Rosenthal, and Henry Lesieur, Ph.D., began to speak out, calling for a new approach to what was happening in the lives of those they saw in their practice and research.

These problem gamblers (also referred to as pathological, compulsive, or addicted gamblers) had something in common in their behaviors that provided a very simple description of their problem: an overwhelming and uncontrollable impulse to gamble. They could not stop themselves from gambling, either by sheer determination of will or by rigid self-discipline.

Largely through the efforts of the late Robert L. Custer, M.D., in 1980 the American Psychiatric Association first recognized pathological gambling in its *Diagnostic and Statistical Manual*. Called the DSM-III-R, it is used to diagnose compulsive gambling behavior, which for the first time in history came to be viewed as a psychological illness.

DSM-III-R CRITERIA FOR PATHOLOGICAL GAMBLING

A person whose behavior meets three or more of the following criteria is considered to be a compulsive gambler:

1. Frequent preoccupation with gambling or with obtaining money to gamble

2. Frequent gambling of larger amounts of money or over a longer period of time than intended
3. A need to increase the size or frequency of bets to achieve the desired excitement
4. Restlessness or irritability if unable to gamble
5. Repeated loss of money by gambling and returning another day to win back losses ("chasing")
6. Repeated efforts to reduce or stop gambling
7. Frequent gambling when expected to meet social or occupational obligations
8. Sacrifice of some important social, occupational, or recreational activity to gamble
9. Continuation of gambling despite inability to pay mounting debts, or despite other significant social, occupational, or legal problems the person knows to be exacerbated by gambling.

In the same way we would recognize that someone suffering the psychological illness of severe depression needs treatment, the compulsive gambler is now seen as a person who is ill and needs treatment to achieve recovery. Like other chronic and progressive illnesses, compulsive gambling, if untreated, ultimately leads to the destruction of the afflicted person.

The DSM-III-R used adult studies to develop its criteria for evaluating the level of gambling involvement. However, researched evidence to date gives us reason to believe that the same criteria can be applied to adolescent gamblers. Many professionals use the DSM-III-R to diagnose an underlying compulsive gambling problem in troubled adolescents who seek help with other problems.

Gambling has become a multibillion-dollar business in the United States. Latest estimates of the handle (the value) of legal gambling that is done nationwide exceeds $250,000,000,000. That's 250 BILLION DOLLARS. To understand the magnitude of that figure, look at it another way. The money estimated to have been spent on gambling is nearly $1,000 for every man, woman, and child considered a resident of the United States. These estimates do not include illegal wagering, which in sports betting alone would add approximately $40,000,000,000.[3]

From these almost incomprehensible figures, we can deduce one thing for sure—there's a whole lot of gambling going on. Although a small segment of the population regards gambling of any kind as morally objectionable or sinful because of religious or personal beliefs, its popular appeal cannot be denied. To understand America's growing love affair with gambling, it is helpful to look at it from the perspective of our culture. Because compulsive gambling does not happen overnight, you might ask, "Well, where does it begin? What are some common experiences we all share that support the idea that America is becoming a nation of gamblers?"

First of all, we are a highly competitive society. Almost all of our leisure time involves competition-based activities. The recreational pursuits we are known for worldwide—major league baseball, National Football League seasons, National Basketball Association playoffs, the National Hockey League—all involve competition at a professional level.

Research suggests that a learning process takes place during early human development that in a sense "trains" people to gamble.[4] As children, even before we start kindergarten, we become indoctrinated in the culture of competition. Our games teach us that the one who collects the most pieces is the victor. The one who beats all the others to the finish line wins the prize. Our status is often determined in our play groups by winning these childhood games.

Males, especially, are awarded position within their groups if they show competitive skills that involve courage, bravery, or independence. (Mark D. Griffiths, who has researched gambling in children and adolescents, theorizes that this factor could explain the significant difference we see between the number of male vs. female compulsive gamblers.) But competition even creeps into seemingly noncompetitive activities like swinging on the playground. A little child can be seen pulling hard on the swing and vigorously pumping to swing higher than all the rest.

Competition in and of itself is not necessarily negative. For example, if you are on a team that is competing for the high school basketball championship, you and your teammates learn cooperation, self-sacrifice, and self-discipline—all character traits that will translate into valuable skills as you reach adulthood.

You have only to view the Olympic Games to see what magnificent displays of human excellence are achieved by the determination, grit, and persistence of the contestants. But competition, especially as stressed by many segments of our society, also glorifies winning. Unfortunately, winning is not seen as just one part of the whole of competition. It is viewed as the reason for competing.

Sad for many young people, but all too true, is the remark attributed to Red Sanders, famous football coach, "Winning isn't everything, it's the *only* thing." That perception is absorbed into our emotional development. We are led to believe that the excitement and good feelings associated with winning are available in no other way than through the competitive process. Playing the game well means an obligation to win. Winning is the goal. Winning means the prize. Winning is good.

What does this message tell you if you are not as athletically talented or scholastically gifted as some of your classmates? It says you can't win if you don't compete. You don't live up to the standard set by our culture. What has been lost is Coach Vince Lombardi's quoted philosophy, "Winning isn't everything, but making the effort to win is." The effort involved is deemphasized in our competitive events and sacrificed to the winner-take-all mentality. If you are not a winner, you can be only one other thing—a loser.

Of course, you don't want to be a loser or even think about being associated with one. So if you can't compete at the expected levels either in the schoolyard or at home, you need to find a realm where you **can** compete and be successful in the outcome. Especially during your adolescent years, succeeding in what you undertake is significant to the development of your identity. To have a niche, to participate in an activity that makes you feel really competent, is a vital part in building healthy self-esteem.

The overt attraction of winning is one reason adolescents as an age group are at highest risk for developing gambling problems. Because of gambling's illusory promise to make the player a winner, and because the adolescent's vulnerable developing ego naturally desires this type of reinforcement, gambling is an obvious activity of choice.

Gambling is competition with the singular focus and purpose of winning. By design, gambling pits the player against the house, against himself, or against the other players. Each state lottery, acting as the house, sets odds against its citizens; a video player gambles on his perceived skill to see if he can accumulate the most points; a bet in the football pool is placed against classmates to win on the point spread of this weekend's game.

Because of our culturally endorsed beliefs about winning, kids who have been raised to view competition as a measure of self-worth are wide-open targets for gambling. If status is the prize of kids' games and our culture recognizes money as a way of measuring status, kids are going to gamble. Kids are not money producers; for the most part, they are money consumers. So, with limited ways to acquire the status symbol of our culture, and with billions of dollars poured into advertising that says gambling can make you a millionaire, kids are going to gamble.

If kids are having trouble at home, if their self-esteem is sliding downhill and school is getting to be a drag and their social life is balancing on the edge of boredom, kids are going to gamble. The developing ego of a fourteen-year-old is pretty fragile, and any activity that seemingly helps to hold it together looks very inviting. For more and more kids, gambling is the ego reinforcement they use to feel like winners.

A second reason gambling is growing among young people is the much discussed peer pressure factor. Unlike some cultures where the beliefs of one's parents or of the community have significant influence on individual behavior, American adolescents seem to be influenced most by their peers. Without your even being conscious of it, the influence of friends begins to impact in earnest on your behavior in your later childhood. The games you play and the risks you're willing to take during those games depend a lot on who's watching the action.

For instance, think back (say when you were eight, nine, or ten) to some of the stuff you did with your friends. You might have told your best friend that you could jump that four-foot-wide rain puddle with only a standing start. Maybe you boasted to your BMX buddies that you could go down the steepest hill in the neighborhood on the back wheel of your bike.

Either of these antics involved a chance that you could fail: You could have ended up with slimy mud on your face or a broken bike and a fractured arm to go with it. But there were your friends urging you on, and you wanted to stand up to their expectations. Because of that peer pressure, and because it was possible that you could do the thing you gambled on, you went ahead and took the chance.

As the years go by, many of you add the possibility of winning money to the things you do with friends. That adds a new element of risk and excitement. Not only do you risk bruising your pride and your body if you fail, you risk losing money—hard-earned money acquired by doing household chores, or on a newspaper route, or saving up from an allowance.

Whereas some kids find it a gut-wrenching experience to bet money on the outcome of a game, others are energized by it. Adding the element of financial risk intensifies the experience for many kids. They quickly learn that wagering in front of their friends is extremely pleasurable. It fulfills their need for attention.

Pressure from your peers to "try it" draws many of you into your first formal encounter with gambling. Peer pressure makes you do many things on the spur of the moment that you wouldn't even dream of if you thought about it beforehand. For instance, going into a store for a soda and trying to buy a lottery ticket without being asked for age identification is a common introduction for those of you who admit to gambling. The "see if you can do it" dare is much the same as it was for your parents when they were underage and tried to buy cigarettes for the first time. The only difference is in the potentially addictive substance of choice.

So, even though peer pressure is nothing new, the way you and your friends are choosing to act out under its influence is new. Because of the excitement gambling offers, more kids are using it as a tool to get attention from their peer group. It's not that most kids are hooked on gambling itself; they love the attention they get while doing it. One young gambler told it this way: "You know, a couple of us were getting into it [sports betting] and we hit and got lots of cash. So others were wanting to see how this was working. And I said, 'This is how you pick 'em.' And it's like, oh wow, I'm getting some attention here. That's really exciting!"

The importance of gambling as an attention-getting device should not be underestimated. Kris, a sixteen-year-old recovering gambler in GA, recalls, "It's not only the money that's a factor. I wanted to be a big shot in front of my friends. I didn't care about anything else. School was a joke. I wanted to be something that I wasn't. I was very insecure about myself."

Unwittingly, parents or relatives have a great deal to do with introducing young people to gambling. Dad's Friday night poker games, Mom's Saturday night church bingo, and the monthly lotto buys are all ways gambling is a part of our culture. Kids see these pastimes as a normal part of family activities. Even Grandma's weekly stop at the numbers man on her way to get groceries isn't seen as abnormal in some families.

Family card games seem to be one of the most universal ways kids learn to place bets. Penny-ante poker, under/over (a blackjack-style game), and penny-a-point cribbage are some of the traditional card games that kids play with their parents.

But parents are modeling gambling to kids in ways unheard of until recently. Increased participation in state lotteries, as well as the proliferation of legalized private business and Indian gaming casinos, are exposing two generations of families to gambling opportunities that didn't exist twenty years ago. Moms and Dads who were raised without gambling are trying it for the first time, and their kids are watching. Parents are talking about going to the track or to the casino as they used to talk about going to the club or taking in a movie. And kids are listening.

Because many of your parents did not have opportunities to participate in legal or illegal forms of gambling as they were growing up, they often fail to understand that gambling could be a problem for their own kids. Whereas they would be pretty upset if you came home drunk or stoned, they might be supportive if you gambled—and won.

Kids say their parents are disgusted if they lose at gambling. Their parents say, "Hey, you can't keep this up." But these same kids also say that if they tell their parents they've won money, Mom and Dad greet them with, "Atta boy, way to go!"

This lack of knowledge and understanding of gambling as an addiction was revealed by parents of a young compulsive gambler. When their fifteen-year-old son was admitted to treatment, they commented, "Yeah, we knew he gambled, but we never thought it was any big deal. We never dreamed gambling could be a problem."

Unwittingly, parents allow their children to become involved with gambling at an early age. One teen in an addiction treatment program tells how he first began gambling:

"I'd be standing there in the store, and she [Mom] would be holdin' my hand. I'd have to stand there to get the dumb ticket, and I just wanted to leave. Later, well, Mom made me buy tickets for her. So I'd buy some for her and then I'd buy mine. Then we'd get into the picking of the numbers and working on a system. And when she'd win, or I'd win, when the number'd hit, [she'd say] 'You're magic and you're special!' She'd say, 'Boy, you gotta be able to do that again'."

Stories abound of kids your age exposed to gambling and even encouraged to gamble in the family circle. Each year, new forms of gambling open up other ways for families to be the training ground for their children. For example, twelve-year-old Peter recalls his first gambling experience with his parents:

"My family is from Missouri, and we have relatives in Wisconsin. Every summer we go to visit them. We spend time fishing on the lakes and picnicking along the river. It's a real family time, 'cause the rest of the year we're all so busy we don't spend a lot of time together.

"This past summer, when we went to visit my relatives, there was a new greyhound racetrack in the town. My aunt and uncle took Mom and Dad and my sister and me out to the track. While we were having dinner, it was cool 'cause we had a table with a little TV so we could watch the dogs racing while we ate. Mom and Dad gave my sister and me some money that we set aside at our table for betting. Every time there was a new race, Mom and Dad let us choose which dogs we wanted to bet on. They'd place the bets, and if our dogs won, we'd get to keep the money. I just kept picking and picking the winning dogs, and Mom said I was 'hot' that day. I got to keep fifty bucks, plus, Mom gave me an extra five for being lucky for her. I can't wait to go back again next year, 'cause I sure can pick the winners!"

Often adolescent males mention that they were introduced to gambling by their father. Ian, a nineteen-year-old from California who gambles heavily, said he began when he was twelve. He lost $15 at a children's poker game. Ian was so upset by it that his Dad taught him how to play, to make certain he would win and not lose.

Young gamblers tell how their fathers first taught them to play ball. Then the dads teach them how to pick teams for sports bets, instructing them about spreads and handicapping. Fathers take their adolescent sons to the track, explaining how to read a parimutuel ticket and the differences between exacta and trifecta bets on horses.

Eric, a young compulsive gambler, remarked, "When I was gambling with Dad, I didn't even know it was illegal. After all, if you're doing something with your father you don't exactly think it may be against the law. Besides, the point spreads are in the local sports pages."

It seems only natural that fathers show a sense of pride and accomplishment when their sons learn the rules of the games and races. One father said, "I'm proud of my son; boy, can he pick 'em. He tells me who I should put my money on now when we're at the track. That kid is hot!" Of course, his son was eating up the attention, because at age fifteen it's very natural to want to keep Dad happy.

But the scary thing about parents encouraging their children to become involved in gambling is what research is telling us about teens who are regular gamblers. A large sampling of New Jersey teenagers in four predominantly middle-class high schools revealed that 54 percent of the kids have gambled with their parents at some time.[5] Another study of young people in treatment for gambling problems demonstrates that excessive parental gambling was related to their children's gambling problems: 50 percent of the kids who had a parent who compulsively gambled were compulsive gamblers themselves.[6]

In general, it is probably safe to say that parents or relatives who introduce their young people to gambling do so innocently. Examples of how families lead their kids into playing the lottery, pulling tabs, or placing bets are:

- As birthday gifts—A third-grader said that on her birthday one lottery ticket or scratch tab was enclosed in her card for every year she had lived. Her Grandma had started the practice when the state lottery began. Since she didn't have a lot of money for presents, she'd buy the grandchild lottery tickets in hope of winning her a million-dollar gift. The little girl said she'd rather have the cash than the tickets.
- With a family football pool—One family had betting sheets made for the Super Bowl Game or World Series and for Sunday afternoon or Monday night football games. Money was collected and put into a pot. The winning bet got the money; the losers had to wash dishes after the game.
- As child-sitter treats—As an incentive for good behavior during grocery shopping, a sitter promised to buy the children lottery tickets on the way home. The "treats" were handed out with "promises" that maybe they would win some money. One mother found out about this when her child complained of not winning again.

- As dinner entertainment—At a three-generation celebration of Auntie's 40th birthday, the dinner party included six children of fourteen and under. Of course, while they waited for the multicourse meal to be served, boredom set upon the children. Uncle Max decided to divert the little ones with a trip to the pulltab box and bought one for each guest. With much ceremony, he allowed each to pick a ticket.

  Each person opened a pulltab, some hastily ripping, some slowly peeling back the paper slots to reveal the results. The children were excited when one was a $10 winner. Then Auntie opened hers and there was a $100 winner before her! Everyone went crazy! They all agreed she was so lucky because it was her birthday.

  The children were absolutely astounded. For weeks afterward nothing could replace the excitement of Auntie's birthday win at pulltabs. Although it was explained over and over that Uncle Max had spent almost a hundred dollars to produce the winner, they still wanted to go do pulltabs again. They were too young to grasp the concept of odds and percentages, and all they remembered was how lucky you can be on your birthday and how easily you can make money gambling.

- As Christmas or holiday presents—One state lottery urged players to buy tickets as stocking stuffers. Unbelievably, they overlooked the fact that kids are the ones who hang their stockings by the chimney with care. So much public outcry arose that the lottery promised not to do it again.

- As birthday party amusements—During a pizza party at a local pizzeria, the guests were given tokens to play the video slot machines. Though illegal, the kids were given their winnings in money because the owner was a friend of the birthday girl's parents. Those same parents wouldn't dream of giving their children an alcoholic drink, handing them a joint, or buying them cigarettes, but they blithely teach their kids to gamble with no thought of possible long-term consequences.

Even schools and teachers have unthinkingly become instructors in how to place bets and wager pocket money. Incidents reported through a gambling information hotline reveal the following gambling activities in schools:

- Bingo math played by sixth-graders for candy prizes to keep them quiet when they had to stay indoors on rainy days.
- High school English teacher placing bets for students on the weekend game between opposing schools.
- Las Vegas nights held as alternatives to drinking on prom or graduation nights. Though many students were under eighteen, the legal gambling age in the particular state, bingo, blackjack, paddle wheels, and video slot machines were played. A concerned teacher called wondering if classes should be inaugurated to teach kids to gamble, because some kids stayed at one game all night, winning all the prizes. They were so intent on gambling that they refused to participate in the dance or to eat at the free buffet.
- Elementary school fund-raiser in the form of a Las Vegas Room along with the usual carnival games

of skill. Children exchanged real money for play money and used it to play on roulette-like wheels and paddle wheels. Winnings were exchanged for prizes.

Granted, these activities seem innocent enough, and for the majority of kids no harm is done. But caution should be exercised by both parents and teachers when planning, promoting, and engaging students in a gambling-oriented activity. Every major study of adult compulsive gamblers reveals that the majority started gambling in late childhood or early adolescence, between eleven and fifteen. Likewise, 70 percent of Gamblers Anonymous members state that they can trace their gambling to childhood.

The number of teenagers who actively participate in gambling is in sharp contrast to the number even a few years ago. California, for instance, authorized gambling surveys before its state lottery started. Three years later, a follow-up study was done. The research, conducted by Durand Jacobs, Ph.D., showed a 50 percent increase in gambling by adolescents, even though it was illegal for those under eighteen to purchase lottery tickets.

Other studies by addiction trend watchers, such as Michigan's Institute for Social Research, report similar findings. Their tenth annual study recently found that illegal drug use had decreased among adolescents, but a documented increase was shown in problems associated with teenage gambling. According to many treatment professionals and researchers, gambling and gambling-related problems will overtake drug addiction as the number one concern during the next ten years.

The reduction in illegal drug use has been brought about through a variety of means. A great deal of social pressure has been brought to bear on young people by community-based as well as state and federally sponsored programs. Also, a change in attitude toward casual drug use evolved because of massive education and prevention efforts conducted in primary and secondary schools in addition to the "Just say no" message aimed at adolescents. It seems, however, that states are just saying yes to legalized gambling, which can be as damaging and life-threatening in its advanced stages as drug or alcohol addiction.

Tremendous social pressure is applied to involve citizens in gambling, with little regard for the consequences, one of which is increased numbers of underage problem gamblers. Joanna Franklin, Program Director at New Directions Addiction Program in Washington, D.C., reflects on what she has seen in her work with adolescent compulsive gamblers during the past thirteen years:

> "I've seen between 1,100 and 1,200 kids treated for compulsive gambling. The youngest in outpatient care was fourteen, and the youngest in inpatient care was fifteen. The problems that kids are having with gambling now haven't changed—debt, crime, family dysfunction. But the number of kids needing help has increased. The speed with which the problem develops seems to have picked up also."

The increase in teenage gambling seems directly related to the increasing number of gambling opportunities offered and the multimillion-dollar marketing efforts that accompany that expansion. Try to find a media expert who will minimize the impact of electronic advertising. With the average teenager spending four to six hours watching television each day, there is certainly a captive audience for the gambling advertisements throughout prime time.

Although state laws prohibit gambling advertising specifically directed to teens, there is no doubt that kids are seeing the messages on their favorite TV programs and hearing the fast-rapping jingles on their rock radio station. A recent poll guesstimate stated that advertisements for government-sponsored lotteries represented the most widely promoted of all the states' programs.

Daily newspapers offer "bingo bug" games, selectively hiding winning numbers throughout their advertising to increase readership. Fast-food chains, the mainstay of adolescent restaurant choices, offer instant scratch-off games and tie in new food products with nationally televised lottery look-alike tickets. Just scratch and win! After all, it's just entertainment. Or is it? Subtly, the message is coming across that there is a way to get something for nothing, to raise some fast cash, and that way is gambling.

Although state lottery advertisements are not directed at young people, it is hard to deny the impact of one recently aired by the Minnesota Lottery. It featured a Yogi bear-like cartoon character who found relief for his winter blahs by going out and buying lottery tickets. The commercial was filled with the pratfalls and sound effects usually connected with the animation in Saturday-morning kid cartoons. Supposedly the appeal was to the general public to follow the bear's example and play the lottery as a way to beat winter cabin fever. It should have been self-evident, however, just who would be most enticed by animation and silly bears—kids! Again, with no messages saying you shouldn't gamble, there certainly are enough messages sanctioning it in very appealing ways. And that is bothering a lot of people who work with kids your age.

Joanna Franklin comments again: "I see kids involved

in more addictive types of gambling than I used to. We
didn't formerly have lottery, as one example, or video
poker machines. But kids are using both for underage
gambling; they're playing like crazy, and they're developing very serious problems."

The traditional wisdom about state lotteries has been
that they don't appeal to the compulsive gambler. The
waiting time between the purchase of a ticket and
announcement of the winning number has been considered too long to encourage irresponsible gambling.
However, statistics show that kids are using the lottery as
an introduction to gambling. When the novelty wears off,
they move on to other types that involve more action or
excitement.

Concern about the amount of gambling teens are doing
also rises out of the proliferation of electronic slot and
poker machines in casinos. You already know how much
video games appeal to kids. It's not hard to find teens
gambling at these machines at any given time. A recent
visit to a Las Vegas casino found eight teenage gamblers
who had been at the video slots for over an hour, despite
a posted underage gambling policy.

Your generation is probably the first to be so thoroughly
immersed in video technology used for entertainment.
What started out as the electronic Pong game in the '70s
grew to the home Nintendo units in the '80s and the
hand-held GameBoys in the '90s. From the shopping mall
arcades to the home PC terminal games to the inter-
active videos and joysticks, you and your friends are
truly computer chip–driven entertainment specialists.
And don't think the gambling industry hasn't been paying
attention.

Population trends are closely monitored by the gaming

industry to gauge future business. The attraction of your generation to video forms of entertainment is being projected into future gaming profits right now. One of the newest Indian nation casinos opened in 1992 and has 1,000 video slot machines. It's not by accident that the industry leaders are pushing states to sponsor video lottery terminals and encouraging Indian nation casinos to increase video slots, video poker, and video keno machines.

There are those who claim that video gambling games are no more enticing to teens than other forms. If that is true, however, why did South Dakota begin screening video lottery terminals with three-foot barriers so kids couldn't play or watch adults play? As one addictions counselor says, "The kids watch the adults go behind the screen to play the lottery like it was some kind of peep show . . . and they can't wait until they can do it!"

For the past fifteen years, you and your peers have grown up on the third of a second blips that mesmerize the player of video games and video arcade machines. This fast-paced, self-absorbed method of recreation presents a new wave of gambling opportunities for a generation accustomed to playing video games for hours on end.

Sound ludicrous? Stop and think for a moment about the video games you presently play. All such games are focused toward the same purpose—to keep you playing and popping coins in the slot. To be sure, there are different pictures on the screen for different age groups: turtles for the youngsters, heroes for the older kids, and sexy ladies for the male adolescents. They all have the same player activity with different computer-generated action. That means that the five- or six-year-old is doing exactly the same thing as the fifteen- or sixteen-year-old;

their mutual goal is seeing how long they can stay on the machine.

Unlike games in which the skills you acquire can translate into other useful applications, the only skill required is the ability to stay on the machine and in the action. Only one outlet exists that can truly duplicate this activity, and that is gambling on video poker, slots, or video lottery terminals.

Alarm about future gambling problems that could arise from early, intense involvement with video forms of entertainment is not unfounded. Mark Griffiths, who has studied young fruit-machine players in England (a form of gambling similar to our video slots), sees a strong correlation between early video games and later video gambling.

The fruit-machine, coin-in-slot games were the most popular with the British teenagers, and the heaviest players were the teenage males. At first the players said they met in an arcade for social reasons, but in reality their playing became a solitary activity, with little communication or interaction between players at machines. They became totally concentrated on the machine. Many of the players said they could stop playing whenever they chose, but for about 18 percent this form of gambling was problematic; that is, they fit the DSM-III-R criteria for pathological gamblers.

Griffiths has urged exploration of American adolescents' use of video machines and video gambling devices because, like the fruit machines in Britain, (1) they are the most popular with teens; (2) human service organizations are reporting more adolescents suffering from gambling addictions, although there is little public acknowledgment of the problem; (3) players have an illusion of controlling the machines while in fact symbols on the screen occur randomly; and (4) players begin playing for something to do or to win but quickly evolve into playing for the sake of playing.

As Ms. Franklin says, kids are playing lotteries and video slots like crazy, and they're having very serious problems.

CHAPTER 3

Who Are the Kids
Who Gamble?

When Doug Van Nispen, the gambling prevention specialist whom you met in Chapter 1, enters a classroom to talk with kids your age about the downside of gambling, he usually asks this question, "Who would like to win the lottery or the football pool this weekend?"

Immediately, hands from all around the room shoot up. Of course, everyone wants to be a winner, especially a BIG money winner. Everybody loves a winner!

Next, Doug asks how many think they could lose their family, go to jail, or commit suicide because of gambling? You can believe that not one student raises a hand to answer that question. Why not?

One reason is that 99.9 percent of these kids, like yourself, don't even know that gambling has a downside. It is a lopsided message that you see on TV, hear on the radio, and read in the newspapers. Gambling is fun . . . gambling is exciting . . . gambling is glamorous . . .

gambling is the ultimate thrill with no side effects, hangovers, or headaches.

Sure, you hear about the family that lost their house because one of the parents blew all their cash in Las Vegas casinos or dropped every last dime at the racetrack. But that was someone else's family, and it happened far away in a place only adults entered. That hard-luck story couldn't have anything to do with you. Or could it?

Unlike the world that existed when your parents were young, gambling today is everywhere. Unless you live under a rock, you're exposed to it many times each day. With legalized forms of charitable gambling, it's quite possible your school band or athletic uniforms were purchased with receipts from pulltabs. Your local hockey rink or new sports field very likely was constructed through the proceeds of a lottery fund-raiser or school-sponsored bingo games.

Not only has gambling been legalized by all states except Utah and Hawaii, but it is aggressively promoted. If you live in one of the many states that sponsor lotteries, it is nearly impossible to go through a day without receiving a message encouraging you to "play and win millions!" Whether you're buying milk or gas, you'll find enticements to gamble.

Adolescents in increasing numbers are responding to these messages, even though state laws prohibit underage gambling. In fact, the teenager who has never gambled is rare. According to a recent survey among Minnesota teenagers, nearly 90 percent had gambled at least once.[7] Kids are flipping sports cards, pitching quarters, betting on cards, playing bingo, betting on sports teams, scratching lottery tickets, and doing pulltabs—all for money.

Arnie Wexler, a recovering compulsive gambler and Executive Director of the New Jersey Council on Com-

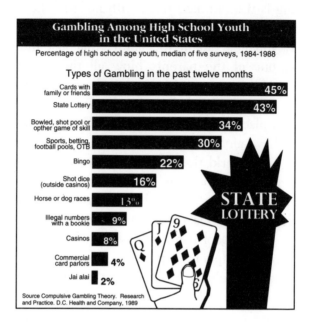

Gambling Among High School Youth in the United States

Percentage of high school age youth, median of five surveys, 1984-1988

Types of Gambling in the past twelve months

Cards with family or friends	45%
State Lottery	43%
Bowled, shot pool or opther game of skill	34%
Sports, betting, football pools, OTB	30%
Bingo	22%
Shot dice (outside casinos)	16%
Horse or dog races	13%
Illegal numbers with a bookie	9%
Casinos	8%
Commercial card parlors	4%
Jai alai	2%

Source Compulsive Gambling Theory. Research and Practice. D.C. Health and Company, 1989

pulsive Gamblers, says, "Wherever kids look, they are hit with messages about gambling. They are told that hard work and an education don't pay off. Winning the lottery, hitting the weekly Pick 6, that's where it's at."

Who are all these kids who are gambling? Take a look around your classroom. If you are between the ages of thirteen and eighteen, it's possible that nine out of ten kids have gambled in one form or another. Studies across the United States show that adolescents are gambling long before they enter high school, with more than 35 percent gambling for money before they are eleven years old![8] Dr. Durand F. Jacobs says, "With one in every ten kids already experiencing serious gambling-related problems, that means two to three kids per class!" Underage gambling is real, it's here to stay, and it is happening in your community.

Teenage gambling takes a wide variety of forms, from placing a wager on the school's Friday night basketball game to playing video slot machines to betting at the track. Some kids bet four or more times a week, and they are having problems because of it. Among the states that have hotlines to assist compulsive gamblers, up to 10 percent of those calling for help are kids under eighteen.

To underline the power of this addiction, Arnie Wexler tells of one teenager who called the Hotline for help. With pain in his voice, Arnie related the story: "This young woman had stolen from her family and sold all her personal belongings to support her gambling habit. Everything of value was gone. The only thing she had left was her body, and she said she would be willing to sell it [as a prostitute] when she needed money to keep her in the gambling action. That's how desperate she was."

Although all adolescents under eighteen (and in some states those under twenty-one) who gamble do so illegally because of state or federal statutory age limits, not all teens who gamble go on to have problems. Take Tessa, for example, a perky, blonde seventeen-year-old junior at a large Midwestern high school:

"I started going to the casino last summer. Some of us tried it just for fun 'cause we were bored. I took along twenty bucks and lost it all doing pulltabs and the slots. I won a couple of dollars too, but it was no big thing.

"I go about once a week now; it's kinda awesome with all the lights and stuff. I get nervous sometimes 'cause I've never been carded for my ID, but I had a friend who was asked for ID. She got thrown out for being underage, and that was scary."

It may be too early to tell whether Tessa will get hooked on gambling. She may just be experimenting with a new behavior as many kids do at her age.

Some kids who try gambling, however, do develop problems with it. Many kids who gamble regularly start at a much younger age than previously thought. Jeremy talked about how he and his friends began gambling at age twelve:

"We had these weekly 'get outs' where we would meet at a hiding place in our neighborhood just to get out of the house and away from our parents for a while. About four or five us would meet and we'd play a three-card game called 31. Those were great times for being together, but we were intense about playing cards. It was almost like we were out to get one another. The tension would always build.

"For instance, we developed our own language that we'd use only when playing cards. A winning hand was called a sh__ sandwich, and the losers were told they had to eat it, which meant pay up. Then too, there was an unwritten rule that you could never walk away from the table if you were a big winner. You would get hassled real bad by the losers to stay and give them a chance to win some money back. It was like a gambling agreement.

"Our game would start out with small stakes, a couple of quarters. But we'd always end up raising the stakes when someone was down. Instead of quitting, the loser would raise the stakes and try to win back the money he'd lost.

"We also had a rule that if somebody was out of money and wanted a chance to try to win it back, somebody would cover him. If you refused a loan to someone who was losing, you were really given a hard time by everyone there. So nobody ever really left the card table without having some hassles. And this was among a group of so-called friends."

The Minnesota survey showed that 6.3 percent of teens who gambled were current problem gamblers. That is, they regularly had symptoms that have been linked to adult problem gamblers. And 19.9 percent of teens between fifteen and eighteen were identified as at risk for becoming compulsive gamblers. These kids gamble in ways that may lead them to have significant problems in the future. Another national study revealed that as many as 13 percent of kids who gamble are stealing and committing other illegal acts.[9]

Jeff is now nineteen, dark and soft-spoken. He didn't know, when he started betting horses at the age of thirteen, that gambling could be anything more than adrenalin-pumping excitement. He knows differently now, and he's paying dearly for what he learned.

"I was in junior high, and I lived in a neighborhood near the track. My dad bet the horses and talked about the fun of watching the winner come racing across the finish line, especially if he'd placed a big bet on it. At first, Dad would take some of my money from my part-time job and place bets for me. He'd bring home my winnings, and we'd split the cash.

"Summer came, and with me out of school and Dad at work, I thought I'd go to the track myself. I don't know, maybe I looked older, but no one stopped me as I went through the gate. The guard didn't stop me at the turnstile, and the man didn't question me at the window when I placed my bets. What a rush it was just to get that far.

"But that wasn't half of the rush I felt when my horse won. Before long, I was at the track from noon to midnight. I was always at the track. If my friends wanted to find me, that's where I was.

"Over the next three years, I gambled all the time. I didn't do well at school and I didn't care. I just wanted to be where I could have some action, and that was gambling at the track. During one seven- or eight-month period, I was going every day. I'd lose $5,000 or $6,000 one week and go back the next week and win maybe $2,000 or $3,000. I'd keep going back, winning and losing, winning and losing. Imagine, a kid doing that!

"I was sixteen, and I sure didn't have that kind of money from any job I held. I borrowed all I could from friends, and I owed everybody. Man, I was so far in debt, but I wanted to keep on gambling. It got to the point where I'd take stuff that wasn't mine and hock it to get cash. It didn't even bother me, 'cause I needed the money for my gambling addiction.

"I started breaking into cars, stealing stereos, breaking into houses, anything to get money to support my habit. Finally, I was caught and sent to jail. I'd just turned eighteen.

"Looking back, I think gambling is as addictive as cocaine or alcohol. Matter of fact, it's worse, 'cause you're not putting something up your nose or down your throat, so you don't even notice you're getting hooked. But I've got to admit it's an addiction 'cause I committed all those crimes just to support my gambling habit.

"I've been gambling-free for six months now, but

I'm going to be paying the rest of my life for my addiction. I figure if I spend half of my salary paying off my gambling debts, it'll be the year 2010 before I'm debt-free."

Teenagers who gamble come from every walk of life, every economic background, every nationality and color. Because gambling is now socially acceptable, and because additional opportunities are offered each year, the profile of the gambler is changing. It is estimated that as many as 7,000,000 underage gamblers nationwide bet for money, and of these more than one million have gambling-related problems.[10]

Popular assumptions, and even early research on compulsive gambling, profiled a gambler as having recognizable characteristics, usually a middle-aged male, white, of lower to middle income.[11] This gambler used bookies to bet on sports, spent his days at the track or nights playing the Las Vegas or Atlantic City casinos. Though many gamblers still fit this profile, fundamental changes are occurring.

With the expansion of Indian casino gambling around the country, an entirely different portrait of "the typical gambler" is emerging. A casino customer is more than likely female, late fifties to early sixties, and has traveled a hundred or more miles by bus. There is one other key change: The face of the gambler is more and more likely to be that of a teenager.

Many of the characteristics that identify adult compulsive gamblers are applicable to adolescents who become drawn to gambling. Normally these "soft" or suggestive signs,[12] as they are called, point to a very successful, motivated young person who could achieve just about anything he set out to accomplish:

- He is intelligent, in the 115–120 I.Q. range or higher.
- He has a high energy level, always ready to get involved, but he is a better organizer than participant.
- He has a history of excellence in athletics.
- His school performance has been good.
- There is a history of steady work performance. He has probably held some kind of part-time job for several years.
- Alcohol or other substance abuse has not been part of his regular behavior.
- He does not have time for hobbies. Work, school, and extracurricular activities take up all his time.
- He has high expectations for himself and others. He's a perfectionist who cannot tolerate mistakes or shortcomings in himself or those around him.
- He is a risk-taker, always ready to meet a challenge head-on, and he admires this quality in others.
- He is bored easily in social settings. Looking for new challenges and new situations keeps him feeling up.

If these traits are characteristic of someone you know who is gambling heavily, he could be headed for a gambling addiction in the future.

The majority of adolescent gamblers are male, but young female gamblers are growing in numbers. Studies show that at least one third of those who have problems with gambling are female.[13]

Because the image of the gambler has traditionally been the hot-shot, smooth talker, females as gamblers have been overlooked. But they are out there; they just gamble differently. Often they gamble alone. They don't boast about their gambling as much as the males do. Sometimes they are even secretive about it because of the double standard society attaches to gambling.

Whereas men who gamble are stereotyped as smooth, smart big shots, women who gamble face a stigma. If a man gambles compulsively, he may be greeted with no more than a societal wag of the head. A female, on the other hand, may be faced with outright contempt as being immoral or indecent.[14]

One reason the number of female gamblers, and female problem gamblers, is increasing is the availability of new opportunities such as the mega-bingo palaces, video slots, and pulltabs. These activities appeal to the female gambler who seeks escape from problems with a boyfriend or parents or who seeks relief from loneliness.

A few years ago, a widely publicized case brought to public attention for the first time just how addicted to gambling teens can become. A seventeen-year-old girl, Debra K., was arrested for underage gambling in a casino. She says, "I was attracted by the excitement. It made me feel important to get dressed up and be treated like an adult in the casino, you know, not like at home where you're treated like a kid.

"My parents had gotten a divorce, so I moved from New York to live with my dad in Atlantic City. I was lonely and homesick for Mom. Gambling was a way to forget all that."

Debra used gambling to escape some of the problems (lack of self-esteem and loneliness) that most teens face. But the consequence of using a potentially addictive behavior as a way to solve problems is *more problems*!

Debra started skipping school and gambling every day. She disappeared for hours at a time. As her addiction progressed, she used up the $5,000 her grandfather had given her for college. She went through her own bank account and lost several jobs.[15] Come graduation time, Debra almost didn't get her diploma. The final blow to her family came when she stole $2,000 from her father.

Debra's father, Leonard, says, "After she disappeared again one night, I went to look for her. I'm a detective cop, so I had some hunches where she might be. I was walking down one street and on impulse went to the casino. There I found her, getting free drinks at some of the best tables.

"I tried to stop her from gambling, and she'd promise to quit. Sometimes she did quit for a while, but pretty soon she was back sneaking into the casino again. It was getting worse and worse. I had to do something."

The "something" Debra's father did was have her arrested for underage gambling. Finally, the secret world she had been occupying in the casino came to light on the front pages of newspapers all across the country.

Debra's story has a bittersweet ending. Now in her early twenties, she and her father are estranged because of what has happened during her addiction to gambling. According to Leonard, she is still gambling. "I've lost my daughter because of gambling," he says sadly.

As a result of Debra's widely reported arrest, Atlantic City casinos have implemented more stringent regulations covering admission to their floors. Harrah's Project 21 uses posters, fliers, and advertising to let kids know that gambling on their floors, if you're under twenty-one years old, is illegal. Trump Casinos recently worked with a group of teens to make a rap video about the consequences of underage gambling. Designed to appeal to the fourteen- to eighteen-year-old, it is an effective educational tool.

But kids are still getting into casinos illegally. In 1990 a casino that has an admittance age of 21 escorted 35,000 underage gamblers off the floor and turned away another 230,000 at the door. An informal poll of 300 Minnesota high school juniors and seniors showed that 10 percent of the class, all under the legal gambling age, were frequenting casinos to play pulltabs and video slots. Common sense tells us that these figures represent only a few of the adolescents across the country who gain access to casino gaming floors.

Michael, twenty-three, is a compulsive gambler presently in treatment. He has been jailed for crimes he committed to obtain money for casino gambling. Michael spoke about his early introduction to casino gambling:

> "I started gambling in casinos when I was sixteen. I lost all my money the first weekend. But the thrill of placing the bets was so exciting. I just couldn't stop. When I was gambling, I was as high as could be. I didn't need anything else."

Michael's gambling drove him to depths of behavior he never thought possible. Neither his parents, school authorities, nor the law could get in his way when his gambling reached the desperation phase. He remembers, "No chemical I ever put in my body ever got me as excited as placing a bet, and I would have killed for it."

Though many of the teens who have problems with gambling live in metropolitan areas, residing in a suburb or rural area does not make you immune.[16] The recent proliferation of gambling casinos in Connecticut and Minnesota and the growing pulltab operations run by charitable and fraternal organizations are targeted to economically depressed rural areas. The profits from these specific forms of gambling are used as revenue for local services and provide much-needed jobs in areas of chronically high unemployment. So even in traditionally isolated rural areas, gambling is now accessible to almost everyone.

Shawn, a nineteen-year-old from a Midwestern town of 5,500, went in one year from being a straight A student to flunking his senior year in high school. His mother called a hotline for compulsive gamblers and their families with his story:

"Shawn has been such a good kid, successful in school, involved in lots of school activities; I don't understand how this could have happened. Once he turned eighteen, he started going to the local bar. He didn't drink because he's not of legal age, but he and his friends would go to play pool and hang out.

"Since he wasn't drinking, we didn't think there was anything wrong with his being there. But what we didn't know was that he and his friends were betting on the pool games in ever-increasing amounts. Pulltabs were sold there also, and since Shawn was of legal age to buy them, he was spending a lot of his money on that too.

"It wasn't until my husband and I returned from vacation that the whole terrible truth about Shawn's gambling habit emerged. He'd been left in charge of our home while we were on a two-week trip. Upon returning, we found several hunting rifles and a pistol missing from my husband's gun collection. When we confronted Shawn, he said they had been stolen, but those guns were under lock and key and there was no way that could have happened.

"When we said we would call the police, Shawn confessed that he had spent so much money betting on pool and buying pulltabs that he sold the guns to pay off some of his debts to friends.

"The next day, the high school principal called to inform us that Shawn had been skipping school while we were gone. He'd been seen downtown gambling. We told Shawn he was never to gamble again, and he promised he was done with that.

"The final shock came the next Monday. The owner of the business where Shawn worked part time phoned to tell us he was pressing charges of theft against Shawn. He said he had more than enough evidence to convict Shawn of stealing cash from the till.

"Our son now has lost the scholarship to college he worked so hard to earn, faces criminal charges of theft, and has jeopardized his future. But why did he do it? And for what—a few pieces of paper, slot machines, and some bets on a pool game?"

The questions raised by Shawn's mother bring to light the need to look at other areas of an adolescent's life when he or she is having problems with gambling. Shawn and his family seemed to be functioning pretty normally, and maybe no one could have foreseen that he would have problems with gambling. However, many researchers find that teens who are having problems with gambling or who exhibit the highest risk for becoming problem gamblers are experiencing other difficulties in their lives.

Joanna Franklin notes that of the kids who enter treatment for gambling problems, almost all come from dysfunctional homes. "What these kids are seeking initially when they try gambling is stability, attention, respect, and affection," she explains. "Besides dealing with their own hormonal imbalance and intellectual immaturity, they have to deal with split parents, alcoholism, physical or sexual abuse—they just want to escape."

If a parent has gambling problems, the entire family is affected. A gambling parent is often emotionally absent as well as physically absent, so the children are left to fend for themselves. Kids from homes where compulsive gambling is present often receive mixed messages about their own value in their family. If a parent is drinking or using drugs as well as gambling, family life can really become crazy. Because these kids have not learned coping skills, they may turn to gambling as a way to handle the stress.

Judi, a recovering compulsive gambler, reflected upon the home she came from and her early introduction to gambling. Her pain from not being accepted for herself as a child was still evident as she told her story. For her, gambling had been the way to carve out her niche in a dysfunctional family:

> "I grew up on a small farm in the Midwest. We were dirt poor, but that wasn't the cause of our problems. My father was an alcoholic. He was probably a workaholic too, 'cause he poured himself into laboring during every waking hour. When he was home, he was drunk; if he wasn't home, he was working.
>
> "My mother was one of the world's best codependents. She'd complain and whine about my father's drinking, and they'd have horrendous fights. Yet on the weekends she'd be having a beer right along with him. She'd complain about how bad her life was and about the fact that she'd never had any money. She had been an orphan and was from a poor family.

"Even though Mom had to raise six children mostly by herself, she worked outside our home full time. I came along twelve years after my sister, born late in my mother's life. Mom never hid the fact that basically I was a surprise, a mistake, and wasn't wanted. I was often openly resented by her, and she made no attempt to show me affection. She was cold and distant. I guess you could say we never bonded.

"I was Dad's special little girl, the favorite, probably because I was the baby of the family. But unless he was drinking, he didn't pay attention to me either. It was when he was drinking that he said I was the greatest kid he had.

"Though both my parents were working, we never seemed to have any money. Of course, that's most likely due to the drinking and gambling. Money meant a lot to Mom, and she saw to it that we learned our family's value system at a very early age: The only way to measure your value is by the thickness of your wallet. It didn't hurt if you had good looks, but the bottom line was how many dollars you had in your pocket.

"At a very young age, maybe five, I remember experiencing a change in the way I felt about myself. Our house was pretty marginal by today's standards. We didn't have a bathtub or shower, so we washed in an old barrel-like tub. Looking back, I don't think Mom paid any attention to how often we kids bathed. At the most it could have been once a week. Anyway, I remember one day being called in front of the kindergarten class and the teacher pointing out what a dirty little girl I was. She grabbed me by the hair and told the other kids that 'this' was how not to be. 'You go home and tell your mother to wash you, and if she doesn't, you can't come back to this school anymore,' she screeched at me.

"As if that wasn't enough to humiliate me, that teacher marched all the children past me and had them look at my dirty ears and hair. I remember thinking that I wanted to die.

"You know, as a young child, you don't differentiate yourself from your family. In a dysfunctional family that is even more true. You keep the family secrets, and even though you are a little kid, you think it's your responsibility to keep the family together when it's falling to pieces. I became very enmeshed in my father's gambling and alcoholism and my mother's codependency.

"As I look back, I realize I've always been overweight, and I believe even as a child it had to do with my feelings of guilt. Mom didn't like me; therefore I assumed something must be wrong with me. I was rejected by my teacher and subjected to verbal cruelty. I'm sure I felt embarrassed and humiliated, even though I may not have recognized the feelings at the time. But I began to stuff my feelings way down inside, and I began to stuff myself with food to hide Judi away from all the painful realities of life.

"Then there were the weekend gambling binges. Every Friday night, into the house would come the cases of beer, the relatives, and the cards. And out would come the money to gamble! I'm not talking penny-ante poker. I'm talking big pots; maybe $500 would change hands in one evening, and this would go on all weekend. It would get loud, messy, and abusive. But, not knowing anything else, I thought it was the normal way families functioned. That's because I didn't have any real friends outside the family.

"Oh, I was starting to be very popular with my peers, but that was because I was acting out in negative ways in school. I was the joker who made everybody laugh—everyone, that is, except my teachers. As the class clown (and sometimes the scapegoat), I'd do anything to get a laugh, and I totally ignored my education. But I think the acting out was my survival technique, because I used it at home too. I was accepted because my family thought I was funny.

"They also thought I was lucky. Having good luck was another trait our family held in esteem. I frequently played a card game called Smear with my cousins, and I always seemed to beat them at it. Funny and lucky—two very good attributes that, at the time, seemed to help me survive in my crazy addicted family.

"I started baby-sitting at age eight; I was put in charge of my older sister's kids. I grew up fast after that. I began to earn money, and after a few years I was invited to the poker table during the weekend gambling and drinking binges.

"That was significant, because the rule was that kids were not allowed to play cards with adults. Kids didn't have money. But when I was fourteen, I guess they thought I had enough money to buy a seat at the table for at least a few hands. Not only that, I was allowed to play partners with Dad.

"You can't imagine my feelings when I got to be Dad's partner. Man, I was so proud to be sitting at the table gambling with him. He doled out the positive strokes about what a good player I was becoming. He bragged to the relatives about how well I played poker. It didn't hurt either that he considered me the 'lucky one'. In my family, if you were lucky, you had status, and I was 'lucky Judi' to Dad—his lucky charm.

"Meanwhile, my school days were in chaos and I was continually getting into trouble with the staff and teachers. At age sixteen I got pregnant, dropped out of school, got married, and had my first child. My husband was shipped off to fight in Vietnam during our first year of marriage, so I continued to live at home with my folks.

"I really became isolated from any friends I had. Kids my age were all out on dates, going to movies and the prom, while I was living in my parents' home with a baby and no husband around. I was lonely, miserable, and had zero self-esteem.

"Because my husband was a soldier, I got a monthly allotment check from the government for me and my baby. All of a sudden, I possessed the most important element in my family's value system—money in my wallet. So my family became my protectors and my only friends. They were now everything.

"My role at the card table quickly changed from child to adult. I learned the adult rules and played so well that I won twice my allotment check. My full status at the table felt great! Dad was proud of me, and I would beam as he boasted about my abilities as a player. I spent my days waiting for my husband's return with a bottle of beer in one hand and cards in the other."

Judi's use of gambling to deal with her boredom, insecurity, and lack of self-esteem as a teenager developed a pattern for her gambling problems during the next twenty years. Now in recovery from her addiction, she can see how her early introduction to gambling, along with living in an alcoholic family, set her up psychologically to become an addict.

To avoid future gambling problems, you need to be aware of family rules or setups that might leave you vulnerable. Sometimes it's not easy to recognize these unwritten rules, but the following are very common.

"We don't talk about that!" This family rule makes being an adolescent even more difficult. The No Talk rule decrees that whatever goes on in the family must not be discussed with outsiders.

If you are growing up in a family that uses fists or words as weapons, the No Talk rule would prevent you from feeling comfortable telling anyone about what's going on. It forces you to avoid problems in any way you can, because talking about the problems would be admitting they existed in the first place.

If you cannot tell anyone about abuse or addiction in your family, you have to escape somehow or act out in some way that, for a while, takes away the pain, shame, or anger you are feeling.

Gambling under these conditions could be doubly dangerous.

"Nothing less than perfection is good enough!" If your family lives by this adage, you quickly learn that there is no glory in second place. Making the varsity team isn't good enough if you are not chosen captain. Although you raised your GPA three points to get a B on your report card, it wasn't an A, so it isn't good enough.

Being loved is essential to growing up healthy. If being number one is the only way you can get attention, you may be missing much of what you need from your family, and you'll look for it elsewhere. And what holds the promise of being a winner everyday? Gambling! When you use gambling to give you that feeling of being number one, you're bound to end up a loser.

Living in a family in turmoil is tough for anyone. Your needs for attention, respect, stability, and affection are fundamental to developing the belief that you are a worthwhile person. Too often, to fulfill these needs, kids from dysfunctional families turn to getting stoned, getting drunk, or having indiscriminate sex. During the past twenty years, it has been well documented that getting stoned and getting drunk can also get you dead. And now, if for no other reason than the reality that the AIDS virus spreads fastest among people who have multiple sexual partners, judgment and restraint must be used when looking to sex as an answer to low self-esteem.

What is left for kids seeking a quick cure for the psychic pain caused by their needs not being met at home? GAMBLING! It's socially acceptable, it's widely promoted, and it has all the glamour and pizzazz that our culture associates with success. In fact, the hype and advertising dollars poured into its promotion make it more than okay to gamble. Gambling is the thing to do, and young people are strongly drawn to it. Whether it is betting on sports or horses or gambling on cards, at the very least the need for recognition is being fulfilled. When kids are gambling, their peers are paying attention to them.

Research with adult compulsive gamblers in treatment programs confirms what adolescent counselors are seeing in their work with teen gamblers. These adults, who all started gambling in their teens, come from many economic and social backgrounds. But they reveal a common denominator: Gambling was a way to handle the pain they felt growing up in a troubled family. Many of the gamblers who went on to have serious difficulties said their gambling started as a symptom of something much deeper happening in their family relationships. Then, when they became hooked, the gambling itself caused the problems.

We know that young gamblers are introduced to gambling by common situations, either with family or friends or through similar cultural experiences. We know, too, that kids with gambling problems and those who are not problem gamblers often give the same reasons for gambling regularly.

We can use REASON as an acronym for the motives that lead kids to continuing gambling behavior.

Relaxation.   Upon ending a busy week, gambling seems a refreshing change of pace and an interesting diversion.
Enjoyment, excitement, entertainment.   It's pleasurable to be with family at a pizza joint playing video gambling machines. It's exhilarating to go for the prize at the family gin rummy tournament. It's as much fun to gamble as it is to go to a ball game.
Adventure, attention.   Playing the video slots in a casino without drawing the attention of security is a challenge. Beating Dad in five out of six races at the track gets his attention.
Socialization.   You can be with your friends while you watch the basketball game you bet on. All the really cool guys are at the major card games.
Opportunity.   New lottery games are offered every few months. Video lottery terminals (VLTs) are available at the mall. Pulltabs can be bought at the pool hall.

Negative feelings. If you feel uncertain about yourself, you feel confident when you win. You can forget about the troubles with your parents. In a crowd of fellow gamblers, you can feel less lonely.

All of those motives are typical of the reasons that problem and nonproblem gamblers give for gambling. But something begins to happen as wins and losses occur for the person who gambles for the motive of negative feelings.

Because he is using gambling to boost his self-esteem, when he wins, he feels great! He gets a rocket-size jump start in the ego department. His life really doesn't seem so bad when winning. But what happens when the losses occur? (And losses inevitably occur; that's how profits are made in the gambling business.)

This negatively reasoning gambler becomes doubtful about his self-worth. If who he is and how he feels about himself are directly tied to being a winner, his ego gets bruised and bumped every time his team loses or his cards turn 22 up. His motive for gambling become focused on repeating the win so he can again feel good about himself.

The more involved the negatively motivated gambler becomes, the more his reasons for gambling change. He gambles to escape the inner pain he feels when he loses; he also gambles to relieve the depression caused by losing more and more money that he doesn't have, and he lies to his family. He wrongly thinks that by winning big and recouping his losses he can recapture that initial boost to his self-esteem. His gambling increases, and he begins the downward spiral that can lead to gambling addiction.

Certain psychological and social factors can raise red flags that say, "Danger ahead." Two indicators that can

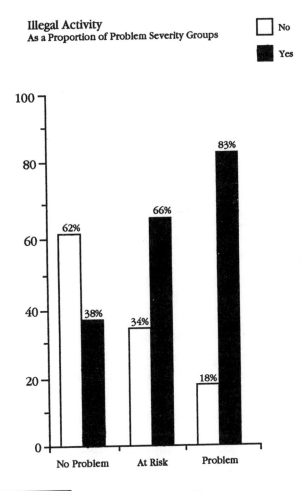

Illegal Activity
As a Proportion of Problem Severity Groups

☐ No

■ Yes

Source: Adolescent Survey of Gambling Behavior in Minnesota.

signal teens out of control with gambling are illegal activities and regular drug use.

The percentage of teens reporting illegal activities when they were identified as problem or "at-risk" gamblers is almost twice that of teens having no problem with gambling (see table above).

From the stories of Jeff, Debra, Michael, and Shawn, who all ended up in serious legal trouble because of gambling, it is easy to see why kids who are considered at risk and problem gamblers may engage in illegal activities. Teenagers in our culture either are given spending money or often have a part-time job. It is the rare teenager who has access to plenty of money. Teens who gamble compulsively increasingly look to illegal means to get the money to support their habit as it spins out of control. At first, they may not even view their actions as illegal, but stealing is stealing, even if the money you take is from your family.

Kris, sixteen, started gambling when he was twelve. By fourteen he was placing bets up to $3,000 a night. He stole from his mother to pay his debts. He recalls, "Gambling deteriorates your home life, wrecks you mentally, eats you up alive. But I'd rather steal from Mom than face a bookie I owed."

The desperation Kris felt as a fourteen-year-old compulsive gambler is powerfully moving. In this state of mind, a teenage gambler would not hesitate to resort to theft to get money to gamble. Just how desperate a kid can become was best expressed earlier by Michael: "I would have killed for it."

The use of psychoactive substances or drugs of any kind (including tobacco) is high among teens identified as at risk or problem gamblers compared to those considered no problem. Whether these teens were using mood-altering chemicals before they started gambling is not known. But what is known is that for some teens selling drugs becomes a quick way to raise money for a gambling habit.

In the strongest sense, kids who are regular drug users and sell drugs to obtain gambling money are utilizing one

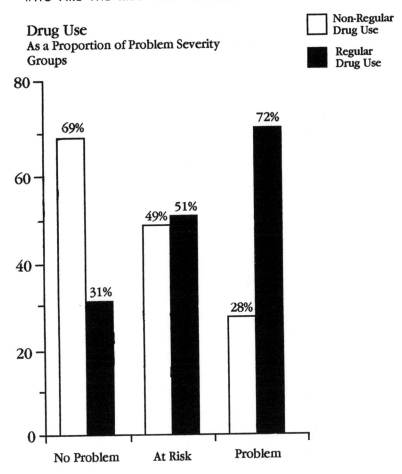

Drug Use
As a Proportion of Problem Severity
Groups

☐ Non-Regular Drug Use
■ Regular Drug Use

Note: Regular drug use is defined as a least monthly use of any psychoactive substance (including tobacco).
Source: Adolescent Survey of Gambling Behavior in Minnesota.

addiction to support another. Because either addiction can ultimately lead to death if intervention or treatment does not occur, the drug use bodes ill for the future of young problem gamblers.

Underage drinking, a more prevalent form of substance abuse, is also connected to underage gambling. One large survey involved 892 eleventh- and twelfth-graders in New Jersey. Forty-six percent of those surveyed said they gambled regularly in a casino, and a substantial percent used a fake ID to get in. While there, 26 percent asked for or accepted free drinks.[17]

Similarly, a survey was conducted at Stockton State College in New Jersey over a three-year period. Among more than 600 undergraduates (half below age twenty-one), almost two thirds were gambling in casinos. Most of those who gambled "usually drank alcoholic beverages at the casino."[18] The most recent data showed that underage gambling students were drinking more than students who were over twenty-one or those who were not gamblers.

The danger of dual addiction for young people increases when you consider that more adolescents are going to casinos to gamble and free drinks are usually offered to gamblers. If you are gambling, you are assumed to be of legal age and therefore are offered drinks.

Is the concern about dual addiction valid? Does the information found in the Minnesota and New Jersey surveys hold up across the country? There is not enough research nationwide to know for certain. However, recent literature shows that substance abusers are at greater risk for developing gambling problems than are other groups. Research in a New York State treatment center for young substance abusers showed that out of one hundred residents, fourteen were diagnosed as compulsive gamblers and an additional fourteen showed signs of problem gambling.[19]

Studies of adults in addiction treatment centers reveal evidence of compulsive gambling and multiple addiction problems. For example, 9 percent of substance abusers in an inpatient treatment program were compulsive gamblers, and another 10 percent showed clear signs of gambling-related problems.[20] And 47 percent of compulsive gamblers under treatment in an inpatient program were also drug or alcohol users.[21]

For adolescents, the possibility seems strong that dual addiction may occur if they start gambling so young. Several reasons exist for this overlapping of addictions:

1. Teens seek a "high" in an attempt to alter their feelings about themselves and their situation in life.
2. Both potentially addictive behaviors often take place in the same social setting and at the same time: drinking and gambling in a casino, using drugs or drinking during card games at a friend's house, pulling tabs and scratching tickets at a bar, meeting the bookie in a pool hall.

Over the past decade, school prevention and education programs have focused on elementary and middle school students. Early education has helped young people understand the danger of potentially addictive behaviors such as drug use, smoking, and drinking. Research shows that this education has paid off in an overall decrease in teenage substance abuse. With increasing evidence of the connection between gambling and other addictions, it would seem wise for schools to implement gambling prevention/awareness programs along with units in existing health and life-style classes.

CHAPTER 4

How Gambling Addiction Happens

J eff, Shawn, Kris, Michael, and Debra, though from different parts of the country and different cultural backgrounds, all have one thing in common: an addiction to gambling. That addiction proved to have devastating effects on themselves and their families.

But how did this addiction come about? Did these kids with above-average intelligence wake up one day and decide that they were going to gamble until they had created havoc in all areas of their lives? Of course not.

Just as none of you would purposely set out to become addicted to drugs or alcohol or smoking, the teens you've met here had no intention of destroying their dreams of a bright, happy future with a roll of the dice or the toss of a card.

Like others their age, these kids who became addicted to gambling may have been trying out new behaviors, testing the limits set by parents and society. When they started, gambling was a fun activity. They saw adults doing something that looked exciting, and they imitated the behavior in an effort to be like adults. Gambling is very seductive to young people, because it promises two elements that are often in short supply during your adolescent years—money and self-esteem.

Money. After all, what is gambling about if not the promise of untold riches? Who hasn't dreamed of winning a million-dollar jackpot? In our culture, a million of anything has a connotation of something really significant, important, and powerful. When we talk in dollars, a million dollars is the ultimate financial goal.

"Tonight, someone could win millions of dollars," the New York Lotto ad reads. "Think of what you would do if you won." Well, lots of kids **are** thinking about what they could do with a million dollars if they won the lottery, and they're trying gambling for just that reason. They believe that instant wealth would change their lives for the better, help them acquire material things, and in many cases even help their families purchase life's basic necessities.

Self-esteem. Teenage gamblers want many of the things money can't buy: respect, adulation, praise, ego satisfaction. They assume that these intangibles will come right along with the million-dollar prize.

If they are winners, they can say, "Look how bright I am; I know how to play, and I know how to win. I've got a system that works. How can I be a loser when I feel like this?"

When Doug Van Nispen goes into a classroom to talk about the choices involved in gambling, he leads his audience through an exercise that helps them visualize how they might react to winning a big jackpot. Using imagination, kids can discover their feelings about winning and discuss whether or not what they perceive fits with the reality of a situation.

"Okay, sit back, rest your arms at your sides. Close your eyes and relax. Take a deep, slow breath; release it slowly. Now, see yourself picking the numbers that you think will win Power Ball. You've got a hunch for the ones that are going to be lucky this time. This is for the big one, the ten-million-dollar jackpot.

"You know these six numbers will work. You feel the fluttering of butterflies in your stomach. Your intuition will pay off this time. It's gotta be right, 'cause you used your system of choosing all the birth dates of family members. Nobody else could possibly have the same combination of winning numbers.

"You have placed your bet. The winning numbers have been drawn. You're sitting here in school, and you are told that your numbers are the winners that came up last night for the ten-million-dollar jackpot! WHOA, what do you see yourself doing now? Are you jumping up from your desk and screaming as you run down the hall? How do you feel? Excited, ecstatic, hysterical? Man, you just won ten million dollars!"

(By now, those working the exercise with Doug are smiling and nodding their heads. Yes, they can see themselves doing that.)

"What would you do next? Would you stay in school? Nah-h-h! Would you find that teacher who's been hassling you about being late and tell her what you really think of her? What about your friends? Would they be giving you more attention than they normally do when they pass you in the hall? How many of them would be wishing they were you with all that money, getting all the high fives. Think you'll be able to land a date for tonight a little easier?

"And that after-school job—would you show up for it today? Well, maybe you'd go just to tell the boss what a jerk you think he is, making you work so hard for pocket change. Now you've won real money, and you can finally tell him where to take this job!

"The same goes for your parents. No more treating you like some kind of infant. You'll decide when you want to leave and when you want to come home. And you'll tell them which sports car you're going to get, 'cause it's your money and your life!"

(By this time, there is a buzz of excited conversation among friends all around the room, elbows jabbing neighbors' ribs, confirming that Doug's description is the way they see their big win happening.)

"Open your eyes and look around. How did winning make you feel? Great? Fabulous, right? But the chance of your actually winning the lotto isn't reality. The odds of winning any particular lottery may be one in a million or even less. Your odds would be ten times better if you dyed one single strand of hair on someone's head purple, and while blindfolded tried to pick out that solitary strand of hair.

"Contrary to what the advertisements would have you believe, winning the Lotto isn't reality for you, nor for hundreds of millions of other folks who put down, and lose, their hard-earned money.

"You're sitting here with your friends, that's reality. Some of you have had a good day, some not so good. But you're here doing what you should be doing to get ahead and be a real winner. You're learning, disciplining yourself through sports, working at your job. Those things pay off for a lifetime. Doing the right thing now is the best sure bet you can place, because you're betting on yourself, not on luck. If you count on luck to get what you want in life, you will be the loser."

During your adolescent years, molding your own identity, defining who you are and where you fit in this world, is called a developmental task. Everybody needs to go through the struggle of self-exploration in order to become a self-fulfilled adult capable of functioning in society. Part of this work of finding out who you are requires you to develop "people skills" outside the realm of your family. Many kids do this by interacting with friends their own age. Gambling sometimes plays a part in this emerging need to have more intense relationships and socialization outside the family circle. That's pretty normal.

For many teens, usually male, one seemingly harmless way to socialize is the Friday night poker or blackjack game with the guys. Parents often condone such get-togethers because they look harmless enough and physically are a lot safer (or so it seems) than a host of other activities their kids could be pursuing on a Friday night.

Coming together to gamble with friends is fun and can give you a real sense of belonging. While playing cards, camaraderie builds. Through conversation about the week's activities—including girls, cars, dates—a closeness develops and a bond is created that may last into adulthood.

Gambling in this way may be seen simply as a diversion, as entertainment in its purest form. The young people get the same pleasure from gambling on cards that they would from going to the movies, watching a football game, or renting a video with friends.

Gambling indulged in for social pleasure is not an abuse or an addiction, and it is the way most adults use gambling. But gambling by anyone under eighteen is illegal in most states. Moreover, if you choose to use gambling as a recreational outlet while you are in your teens, you must be informed about the possible consequences. You're informed about drugs, tobacco, and alcohol; now is the time to become informed about the hazards of underage gambling.

Sergeant Butch Wegman, a police detective, tells the following stories about three teenagers who were members of a winning city-sponsored hockey team he coached. They illustrate how teenagers are significantly at risk for developing a gambling addiction. In each case, the young man used gambling as a major form of entertainment or socialization without understanding the consequences of excessive gambling, and later came to grief.

Todd

"This mid-sized Midwestern city provided the same setting for my son and his hockey friends as it did for me when I was growing up. My son and his friends went to dances and parties, fished, and played hockey. But their future will be different from mine. Something has happened to them, and that something is gambling.

"Todd is the son of one of my old fishing buddies. Todd always wanted to be a policeman, and he is bright enough to do that. I occasionally teach a class in Criminology at the university, and one day I noticed Todd among the students. Because I was his former coach and we were good friends, Todd would sometimes stay after class and we'd talk. About midway through the semester, Todd was arrested for burglary. He was caught in a house by the owner, late at night.

"Now this kid had a completely clean record, no priors at all, and I'm left wondering, how can this be? My first thought was, hey, his career in law enforcement is gone. What will his Dad think about this? The whole circumstance seemed completely out of character. Up to this point, he was a real good kid and I liked him.

"Well, somehow, Todd got his legal problems straightened out and finished the semester with pretty good grades. So I figured, maybe the kid just made a mistake, and I didn't think about it any more—until recently.

"I was transferred into the detective bureau of our police department, and the first week I was here, one of my partners said, 'Do you know Todd? We have to serve a search warrant on his house.' My partner was asking about the very same kid, Todd, son of my friend, and my former hockey star.

"We went to the place where he was rooming in an old apartment house. I went in, and there was his hockey equipment in a corner along with his fishing gear, a bed, a lamp, and some clothes. That was it.

"Todd had no job, and he was spending an awful lot of time out of the city. We discovered that he had made many, many trips to Las Vegas and Reno. On further investigation, we find that he is getting his money by going to small towns throughout the state and doing the same type of home burglaries that he did here. In fact, he is suspected of having committed between thirty and forty felony thefts!

"Todd, who is now twenty-three, is wanted and on the run. He has thrown away his future in law enforcement. He had a beautiful girlfriend, and I know he loved her dearly. But he's lost her too.

"If you could talk to him, you'd like this polite, big, strong, good-looking, clean-cut young man. He had everything going for him, but he's caught in a net of compulsive gambling. He's desperate for more and more money to finance his gambling, so he steals."

Ray

"Ray is another young man I've known since he was twelve years old. He came from a single-parent home and was always an independent sort of guy—free-spirited, kind of a loud mouth. He didn't do real well in school, but he never got in trouble with the law.

"Ray was on my hockey team. He was a good player, aggressive, enthusiastic. When we went on hockey trips, we had to endure a long bus ride. To pass the time, a core group of kids would get together and play penny-ante poker in the back of the bus. Everybody would get in on it and play at some point, but I always noticed that Ray and two others were instrumental in getting the games going.

"Not too long ago, while jogging, I saw Ray. He came walking out of a house and flagged me down. 'Hey, Mr. Wegman,' he said, 'sure is good to see you.'

"He told me he was leaving soon for California,

where the weather would be nicer, and I assumed he had a job and whatever out there.

"Well, I went in to work and one of my partners said, 'You know Ray?'

"'Yeah,' I said, 'I know him well; he's a friend of mine.'

"My partner says, 'I'm looking for him. He's got a whole bunch of bad checks out there.' Then another investigator says, 'Well, I'm looking for him on a case of criminal damage to property. Ray went crazy one night at a fast-food joint and tore the place apart.'

"So I'm really scratching my head on this one. I started to do a little research. Why the bad checks? And why would he destroy property in a restaurant? I approached my son, who knows Ray too, and asked him what was going on.

"'Dad,' he said, 'Ray spends everything he's got on gambling. He's always down at the casino, and he doesn't have any money, so he writes bad checks to get cash and keep gambling. This guy's desperate.'

"Ray is wanted on two separate warrants. I have been friends with this kid for so long that quite frankly, it would be difficult to arrest him. I will—but it hurts me."

Chad

"Chad has long been a neighbor of mine, and he was a good hockey player too. He's the type of guy that everybody loved. He'd fit into any group, anywhere, anytime. Also, he was one of the kids who sat in on the bus poker games.

"Before those games, even at fourteen and fifteen, these kids held poker games at each other's houses, just as their fathers would have. The kids would get together at somebody's house on Friday night. They were even at my house a couple of times. They'd have pop and potato chips, and we thought it was okay 'cause we knew where they were and what they were doing. We didn't know kids could get addicted to gambling.

"Anyway, after hearing about what had happened to the other guys on the team, my son says to me, 'Dad, did you hear what happened between Chad and Davey?' It seems Chad had called Davey and asked for $1,000 real, real quick because some people were after him. He promised Davey he'd pay him back in a week or two after he had sold his car.

"So they struck a deal. But that was six months ago, and nothing has been paid back. After pressuring Chad, Davey learned that Chad's in debt for $40,000 or $50,000. He's on the run from some bookies he owes for sports betting. He's in a lot of trouble with some people who seriously want to hurt him, and he's scared to death."

At this point, Sergeant Wegman just shook his head. "The sad part of it is that these young men are my friends, and now I've got to deal with them from a legal standpoint. They've all gotten on the bandwagon of gambling and don't know how to get off. They've ruined their futures. To end up with a criminal record, not to finish school, to lose the woman you love, to be tens of thousands of dollars in debt with nothing to show for it—and all because of gambling."

When I asked Detective Wegman what could be done to prevent others from having gambling problems, he answered, "Have parents, schools, and the governing bodies that sanction gambling say to young people, 'No, you must not gamble, it's not all right, it's not acceptable behavior at your age. Life-changing consequences can be involved.'

"Very few warning messages are coming from those in the business of gambling, including most states. If we are mute on the issue, we are in effect condoning it as acceptable behavior for kids. We know so much more now than we did just a few years ago when these young men were adolescents playing poker in basements and on the bus. It's time we speak out and give kids some standards against which to measure their behavior, just as we've done with smoking and drinking and drug use."

CHAPTER 5

What the Gambler

Seeks

Many kids tell us they started gambling because
they were bored and wanted a diversion from
their everyday routine. Gambling is only one
activity teens can choose that offers excitement to its
players. But, because of the proliferation of gambling
outlets in this country, it is becoming a major diversion
used by teens for excitement. The marketing of the
industry certainly makes gambling look exciting. (Have
you ever seen a lottery commercial promising quiet times
and serenity?)

The need to play, to create an inner sense of excitement doesn't end as we grow from childhood to adulthood. We just change the ways we act out the need for
excitement. All this searching for excitement is positive,
because the feelings it produces tell us we are really alive.
We feel the butterflies in the stomach, the tingling of the
skin, and quickening breath as a physical response to the

mental function of being excited. It's a complex process, one we all want to experience and repeat.

A friendly game of cards with the guys can be exciting for some. As the cards are dealt and the bets placed, pulses quicken, jaws set, neck muscles tense, and palms sweat. Who will hold and who will fold? Until each hand is played out, nobody knows.

Though the amount of money lost is usually not great, the unknown and the anticipation create an excitement that young people seek. Many students report losing from five to twenty-five dollars in an evening. That amount corresponds to what they would have spent if they had chosen another form of entertainment to break their routine on a weekend night.

The need for excitement may be fulfilled in a slightly different way with kids who play the lottery weekly. For instance, a teenage girl and her friend go to the convenience store to buy snacks and fill up their car with gas. They may spend three to five dollars on lottery tickets or scratch tabs. The excitement comes in two parts for them. First is the rush of wondering whether they will be refused when they approach the cashier, whether or not they will be caught. Second is the possibility that they'll win $1,000, although the odds may be 500,000 to one.

Risk is involved because at sixteen the girls are under the legal age in all states for buying a lottery ticket; they may be spotted by a clerk who is trained to check identifications, then told to leave.

If the girls do avoid notice and buy a couple of tickets, the excitement continues to build as they scratch off the film hoping to reveal a winning combination of symbols. Even if they don't win the big prize, they think, maybe they can win a few dollars that will pay for admission to the dance tonight.

Whatever the outcome, there's the fun, the excitement, and the diversion provided by gambling, plus the social contacts made and the pleasure of just hanging out with friends. These teenage gamblers would fit the description of an adult **social gambler**.

A social gambler is a person who has a casual acquaintance with gambling. Usually, the gambling is done with friends or family. The social gambler may gamble as seldom as once a month or as often as once a week. The gambling is done for relaxation and even distraction. It is engaged in simply to break the predictability of daily activities and to experience a little pleasure with people whom the gambler enjoys.

Social gamblers often set an amount they'll spend on their diversion. Like a budget for any other recreational activity, they decide on a small sum that they are willing to spend (lose) on gambling. Though a possibility exists for winning money during the evening, that is seldom the reason for playing. The stakes may be so small as to be insignificant. Rather, it is the camaraderie that is the real payoff for the social gambler. In fact, if gambling were eliminated from this person's life, other social pursuits could just as easily fill the need for excitement and companionship.

One school of thought views excitement as the gambler's drug. Nothing is taken into the body that causes the addictive behavior to develop, so the addiction is not physical; it's psychological. It is the promise of excitement that eventually gets the gambler hooked.

The level of excitement experienced by compulsive gamblers is called "action." Action can best be described as a high similar to the euphoric state experienced by users of cocaine or amphetamines.

One young gambler explained being in action this

way: "As we played cards and the stakes kept getting higher, I watched my friend get more and more hyper. He'd start bobbing his head up and down, rocking back and forth faster and faster. Then he'd start banging his hands on the table like it was a drum and tapping his feet on the floor. He'd laugh and giggle hysterically, as if he was using speed [an amphetamine] or something."

Recovering compulsive gamblers have said that the excitement they felt when gambling was like nothing else they had experienced. And the price they paid for achieving excitement through gambling was higher and more devastating than they could ever have imagined.

Everywhere, kids are bombarded with "feel good" messages from a world focused on instant gratification. Any activity that appears to offer escape from the tension and turmoil of just being an adolescent looks pretty inviting. Worrisome home situations, rejection by a boyfriend or girlfriend, anxiety about grades and home-work can all weigh heavily on you. When you view television commercials for casino gambling or state-sponsored lotteries, you see people who are **happy** and thus apparently worry-free. What an enticement! Why wouldn't a teenager want that same emotion in his life?

The initial euphoria that gambling gives some people may be a shockingly pleasant experience. Most kids know that gambling will not solve all their problems, but they find out very quickly that it can provide momentary relief and escape.

One young gambler had left her family and gone to Las Vegas to get away for a while. Upon entering a casino and seeing all the different gambling games, she had one thought—Where has this been all my life? The effect on her was so incredibly powerful that she didn't want to go home.

Gambling is fast and simple—important requirements when short-term relief is sought to avoid facing troubles head-on. If a gambling experience substitutes good feelings for bad, more than likely it will be tried again the next time a quick pain reliever is needed. This kind of gambler is called the **escape and relief** gambler.

The psychological addiction develops as the gambler returns over and over to the behavior. Especially for young persons who lack the knowledge, ability, or opportunity to derive pleasure from other sources, gambling indeed becomes a risky behavior.

As time goes on and gambling is more frequently pursued for relief and escape, a psychological change occurs in people. Now they become unhappy and depressed if they cannot gamble, and the only way to escape these uncomfortable feelings and reduce the building anxiety is to gamble again. But gambling no longer is a way to get relief. Gambling becomes the *cause* of their need to seek relief from the problems it develops. When this happens, people will do whatever is needed to get the "drug," gambling. They have lost control and are addicted.

If you think about it, gambling used in this way is much like alcohol. You could substitute the word "drinking" for "gambling" with teens who use it for relief and escape. This provides a perspective on the addictive qualities of gambling and the reason for concern about those who resort to gambling as a way to relieve the tension and pressure of everyday life.

Unlike adults who may have learned stress reduction exercises and problem-solving techniques, kids are in danger of building a dependency on gambling when they use it to avoid dealing with problems.

The majority of studies of adult compulsive gamblers show that they started gambling in their early teens.[22] Looking back, one recovering compulsive gambler reflected, "I know I started gambling to escape all the fighting between my parents and the drunken stupors of my mother. I could just as easily have used alcohol as a way to avoid the unpleasantness of my home situation, but I already knew I hated booze because of what it did to Mom. Gambling with my friends looked like a pretty harmless way to take care of my feelings of inadequacy and shame."

If over the past two months you have increased your gambling or found yourself using gambling as an outlet for your frustrations, now might be a good time to do a self-check. As honestly as you can, and just for yourself, answer these questions:

- Why did I first try gambling?
- What is my reason for gambling now?
- What feelings about myself does gambling enhance?
- What feelings about myself can I suppress when gambling?
- Which description of gambling style—social, or relief and escape—fits me best?
- What three positive things can I do to release tension?
- If I quit gambling, what other recreations could I try?

So where is the line drawn between gambling as purely a social activity and as an addiction? How can you tell if your gambling, or that of someone close to you, is heading in a downward spin, closing in on the possibility of self-destruction?

Unfortunately, the boundary between heavy social gambling and the more serious abusive gambling that can lead to compulsion is not clearly marked. Like an alcoholic reflecting on his disease, not knowing exactly when the addiction took over, a compulsive gambler might find it difficult to look back and say, "Oh yeah, that's where I crossed the line from being a social gambler to a compulsive gambler."

Rather, the development of compulsive gambling is a gradual process. You may not even notice how often you return to gambling to find solace, reassurance of your self-worth, and momentary diversion from problems. Little by little, the gambling causes its own problems by demanding more of your money and time. Very slowly you drift into the downward swirl toward compulsive gambling.

Maybe you have doubts about whether you or one of your friends could become addicted to gambling. Gamblers Anonymous has developed a list of ten questions for teenage gamblers. If you answer yes to three or more, you may have a gambling problem.

1. Have you ever stayed away from school or work to gamble?
2. Is gambling making your home life unhappy?
3. Is gambling affecting your reputation?
4. Do you gamble until your last dollar is gone, even your busfare home or the cost of a burger and Coke?
5. Have you lied, stolen, or borrowed just to get money to gamble?

6. Are you reluctant to spend "gambling money" on normal things?
7. After losing, do you feel you must return as soon as possible to win back your losses?
8. Is gambling more important than school or your job?
9. Does gambling cause you to have difficulty in sleeping?
10. Have you ever thought of suicide as a way of solving your problems?

The danger of becoming addicted to gambling seems to be especially critical for those kids who gamble for relief and escape. Recent research supports the inherent danger of gambling this way.

Dr. Durand Jacobs, a psychotherapist and one of the handful of researchers who have studied teens and gambling nationally, has developed a general theory of addiction that uses compulsive gambling as its prototype. The theory looks for the commonalities among addictions that point to their being treated as a unified class of behavior.

Dr. Jacobs theorizes that all addictions have a reinforcing quality that keeps the addictive behavior going. That is, while participating in the behavior, the person finds escape from painful reality and experiences wish-fulfilling fantasies, such as being important, highly successful, intelligent, powerful, and admired.[23]

As an adolescent, you are in a stage of development that sometimes involves fantasizing as a normal part of creating your sense of self. The allure of gambling and the illusory vision of success it offers play into the magical thinking of teens. "If I win, I'll be popular. I'll have lots of money, and people will like me better." This magical thinking makes gambling very attractive.

With more gambling outlets being opened each year, the increase in the number of teens developing gambling problems is a reality. In the past for most teens, becoming addicted to gambling was not an option. Only a few came upon it and experienced the euphoric results. Not so now. As Dr. Jacobs contends, "Gambling is the addiction of the '90s. If you're sitting in a classroom of thirty kids, two or three of them are already experiencing serious gambling-related problems."

A gambling addiction requires rearrangement of your priorities and time. Before becoming compulsive, a teen gambler looks pretty much like anyone else in this age range. This fictitious youth—let's call him Joe—is fifteen and uses gambling for entertainment or as a social outlet. When Joe first starts gambling, his twenty-four-hour day looks pretty much like that of any other normal teen.

Eight Hours School. This usually includes travel time plus time for a couple of snacks and a burger at lunch.

Six Hours Sleep. Maybe a cat nap is grabbed during study hall, but on average Joe gets somewhat less sleep than he should. That is to leave time to participate in all his extracurricular activities and recreations.

Ten Hours Miscellaneous. Personal care, hairstyling, and general grooming take up goodly chunks of the body-conscious adolescent's time each day. A large portion is spent practicing team sports, working a part-time job, or hanging out with friends. A few minutes are squeezed in with the family over a meal. And don't forget phone time with friends, dating, movies, videos, or time spent just cruising after school. Although he doesn't gamble every day, he probably spends several hours gambling with the guys before or after school.

That is how gambling starts in the lives of most people—a small part in the daily routine. It is just recreation time or relaxing time. It does not interfere with the other activities of life, and most people who try gambling may never have a problem because of it. But for others, the rush they get from gambling is so seductive that their involvement increases immediately. The time demand grows as they become preoccupied with thoughts of gambling. Then too develops the ever-present need to find more money for gambling.

For example, John, a nineteen-year-old Gamblers Anonymous member from California, admits that his gambling stole a "normal" teenage life from him.

> "When I started gambling, I found one of my friends was going to the track a lot. So we hooked up with each other, and pretty soon we were there every couple of days. I tried to juggle my schedule around football practice, but I couldn't always make it back from the track on time and began to miss a lot. It wasn't long before the coach kicked me off the team, but I blew it off, telling my parents that I was cut from the team lineup.
>
> "Then my grades started sliding because, let's face it, I wasn't spending much time in school. Vegas wasn't all that far from where we lived, so my friend and I started driving out there four times a week. Finally, I dropped out of school 'cause I was gambling heavily. I told everyone I planned to gamble for a career, that was my goal, my plan.
>
> "My parents and I couldn't get along anymore. I

was always out late and leaving early to gamble. I was worried about getting more money to gamble, afraid I wouldn't get it, and planning when I could next go. I pawned everything I owned, and I stole stuff from my parents. Then I went to Vegas and gambled. I had no idea how long I was there, but I was told later I had gambled straight through for three days and nights. Anyway, coming home from Vegas I must have fallen asleep, and I flipped my car. That was when I bottomed out. I realized gambling had literally taken over my life."

As you can see, for the person who begins to use gambling in problematical ways, everything else in life begins to get shoved aside. Look at the changes in Joe's twenty-four-hour day when gambling takes over:

Four Hours School. Joe doesn't spend much time in school anymore. His grades naturally begin to slide. He tells his parents that the work is just too difficult, and he can't keep up. He often arrives at school early to play cards, or he goes to the pool hall to play and bet after school. He skips lunch and uses lunch money for gambling, or he uses the time to collect bets from other kids in order to make more money for himself to gamble.

Four Hours Sleep. He's out late gambling night after night. When he's not gambling, he's trying to figure out how to win back what he has lost during the day. He's becoming jumpy and irritable and is unable to sleep when he finally calls it a day—too full of worry about being caught by his parents and not being able to gamble again. At the same time, he's filled with remorse about all the lying he's doing and being unable to level with them about what is going on in his life.

Sixteen Hours Miscellaneous. This portion of Joe's life has been pretty well emptied of the teenage activities he used to enjoy. The coach dropped him from the team for missing practice so often. His part-time job is on the skids, since he's been calling in sick regularly. Then, too, one of his coworkers tipped him off that the boss suspects him of stealing cash after he "borrowed" Friday night's receipts.

Joe's only friends are the few he met through his sports betting activities and the floating poker game. They're not so much friends as potential sources of money for gambling. The old gang he used to hang around with have deserted him. They long ago tired of his constant requests for loans and failure to pay back the money he owes.

And forget the family. Whenever they're together, they fight over the time he's away from home and the trouble he causes at school. He feels shame over the money he took from his little brother's bank, but hey, he'll pay it back soon.

Unless Joe gets help, he's headed only one way, and that's down the hill to a gambling addiction.

CHAPTER ◇ 6

Compulsive Gambling as an Illness

When recovering teen gamblers come together at a Gamblers Anonymous meeting, they sometimes discuss how their gambling progressed to the point of being totally out of control. Lifting the veil of secrecy that kept their addiction going, they begin to comprehend how their actions led to the addiction.

Glancing around this support group, you would see lots of nodding heads as the teens relate to one another's stories. These kids may initially be strangers to each other and come from very different backgrounds, but they recognize the similarities in how "it" happened. The "it" they refer to is compulsive gambling.

If you consider compulsive gambling as an illness, a psychological illness, you can begin to understand why recovering teen gamblers recognize so much of themselves in each other. Although compulsive gambling may be more complex in its development than a physical illness, it does have predictable stages.

For example, if you find yourself sneezing and coughing with a tickle in your throat, you may suspect you are coming down with something. Then if your eyes start to water and your nose begins to run, and a slight fever develops, you can say with quite a bit of confidence that you have a cold.

Compulsive gambling, too, has stages of progression. These stages form a predictable pattern from beginning to end, with symptoms that are recognizable and behaviors that foreshadow the onset of gambling problems. Unlike the flu or colds among teenagers, compulsive gambling is not all that common yet, but its incidence is increasing. Understanding the progression of the illness can help prevent "it" from happening to you.

Two points need to be made about the addiction called compulsive gambling.

1. Unlike a cold virus, compulsive gambling is not a disease that you can "catch" from someone. You don't get it just by coming in contact with gambling people or activities. It involves learning the rules and intricacies of gambling from family or friends. It requires the expenditure of energy, resourcefulness, money, and time. It involves a complicated networking of events and actions over an extended period. In other words, you've got to work at it.

2. You must have a predisposition toward addictive behavior.[24] Teenagers who become compulsive gamblers have a combination of personality traits and temperament that makes them vulnerable to addiction. Their outlook on life could be summed up in a phrase, "Get outta my

face!" They lack a sense of trust. They are unable to develop intimacy with others. Somewhere in their childhood, they received messages that left them feeling unloved, unwanted, and unimportant.

A teenager who is developing an addictive personality may come from a home in which one or all of the following are common:

- Parental abuse, either physical, verbal, or emotional
- Neglect of the child's needs
- Rejection of or indifference to the child
- Emphasis on money and the power or prestige connected with it
- Gambling, drinking, or drug use.

An adolescent in such a home will be impacted by the parents' excesses and be at higher risk of developing problems. A recent health survey in four California high schools examined the environments of teenagers who were users and nonusers of addictive substances. The children who had gone on to become teenage users reported significantly more parental problems than those who were nonusers.[25]

A teen who comes from a troubled home lacks the skills to develop meaningful relationships. Not only is he mistrustful of others, but he tells himself that he doesn't need anybody. He doesn't know how to share his feelings or develop true intimacy. The wishes of others are ignored; he operates on the philosophy that he can do whatever he wants whenever he likes. Anyone in authority is seen as a roadblock to getting his way.

Slowly, imperceptibly, his actions begin to reinforce the belief system he has formed about the world: Life stinks, people can't be trusted. He seeks activities that he thinks will attract the praise, approval, and recognition he so badly needs.

Now, all of us would like to go through life with the fewest possible hassles. But the reality is that setbacks and frustrations must be dealt with. A person who is susceptible to developing addictive behavior, however, does not want to face the little disappointments that come up each day. He wants no pain and lots of gain. Because he has not learned to form trusting relationships with those who should be supportive (usually his family), he is fearful and suspicious of others.

Such a teenager has been taught by those closest to him not to count on human relationships to help him with problems. Coming from this background, he needs something to control, to manipulate that will help him feel in charge of his life. Looking not for the power within, but at the outer world, he begins to move toward activities that he perceives will bring him admiration or acceptance from his peers. He looks outside himself to find projects or adventures that will draw attention and, he hopes, friendship from others.

With all the activities available to a teenager, card-playing, sports betting, and video slot machine playing might seem harmless to anyone untrained in the field of gambling addiction. The young gambler's behaviors (mood swings, secretiveness, defensiveness) may even be perceived as a normal developmental process—just another example of the hormones kicking in! But if a young person has vulnerabilities that make a potentially addictive behavior like gambling attractive, a progression of events begins to evolve that is not normal at all. These are called the phases of compulsive gambling.

CHAPTER 7

Phases of

Compulsive

Gambling

The careers of most compulsive gamblers have three clearly differentiated phases: the winning phase, the losing phase, and the desperation phase. First discussed by Dr. Robert Custer in his pioneering work with compulsive gamblers in treatment, each is a distinct stage through which the gambler passes.

But before even the initial phase, the winning phase, is entered, an introductory or preparatory period occurs. This happens while the teenager gets acquainted with his new interest. Quite often, parents or relatives provide the introduction to gambling. The young person who has not been particularly successful in developing interpersonal relationships begins to develop a relationship with the event of gambling. (The compulsive gambler is referred to as "he" because most teenagers who are identified as compulsive gamblers are male. However, the description could fit a person of either sex.)

Most familiar addictions involve a relationship with a substance. The overeater is addicted to food because while eating he or she feels safe and secure. When the alcoholic and his buddies drink, he feels a sense of belonging to the group. With gambling, there is no substance to ingest, but the relationship to the activity develops just the same.

The association with the event of gambling starts out much like a relationship between two people. The young gambler learns that when he is gambling he feels better. He discovers that gambling can be trusted to put some excitement into his life, especially when he wins. If he loses at this get-acquainted stage, it's no big deal because the relationship he is forming has provided some excitement. While gambling, he feels strong, assured, in control—all the things he doesn't feel in his day-to-day existence.

Young teens who go on to gamble compulsively are at a stage of life that makes them especially susceptible to using gambling in a relational way. During early adolescence, they often look to someone or something else to change the way they feel. Kids whose needs for closeness and safety have not been met by others may turn to an object or event to fulfill those needs. If they become acquainted with gambling, they are wide open to gambling problems. Life can be tough in the early teens; emotionally, life is a roller coaster, and gambling becomes a tool to keep it on track. For instance, the young person who begins experimenting with gambling may be feeling down or depressed. By gambling, he seeks to change his mood, to go from negative to positive feelings about himself. Gambling becomes an antidepressant used to stimulate his emotions, to help him feel up when his world starts to get him down.

Other characteristics that make him vulnerable to the allure of gambling are:

- **Fragile ego**. He easily feels rejected. No matter what he does, he perceives himself as being disapproved of by his parents, teachers, or peers.
- **Impulsiveness**. He leaves one pursuit and turns quickly to another. If one activity is not working out, he drops it and moves on to something totally different.
- **Overanxiety**. He's up one minute and down the next. A change of mood can occur within seconds.
- **Low tolerance for frustration**. He thinks he knows what he wants, and he wants it NOW! Immediate gratification is the goal, and "Why wait?" the motto.
- **Sense of omnipotence**. Because he wins most of the games he chooses, he believes he has the "magical" touch. He's the lucky one among his friends, always slipping by just in time. He avoids getting caught in rule-breaking escapades and believes it's because he's luckier and smarter than the rest.
- **Unlimited energy**. Like the bunny with the battery, he just keeps on going. When his friends call it quits for the night, he's the one who wants to stay out for just one more hour and play just one more round.
- **Risk-taking**. He is always the first to try something new. As a kid, he was probably the one who crawled out the window to the tenth-floor fire

escape just to prove he wasn't afraid of heights. His search for excitement drives him through what he considers an otherwise boring life.

A young person whose personality fits those descriptions is attracted by the lure of gambling and is vulnerable to using it in an addictive way.

Rick, a talkative fourteen-year-old from Wisconsin, has been gambling for a couple of years. He says a lot of his friends gamble, but nobody has problems with it and he doesn't see any harm. Rick is in the introductory stage of gambling activity and is eager to talk about what that is like for him.

"I like to gamble. It's one of the most exciting things I do. I also enjoy football, and I bet on the games with my friends and my dad. We bet on football boards together too. Usually my bets are about $5.

"My father was disabled by an injury, so he's been out of work for a long time. To raise cash, he sells numbers on football boards. Sometimes he has his own boards, and sometimes he sells for a bookie friend of his.

"It was Dad who taught me to gamble. Every fall since I was in seventh grade, he buys my younger brother and me numbers for the Packers' games. Then on Sundays we sit together and watch the game. I always have a great time, and it's gotten so I really look forward to Sundays when football season rolls around.

"I think overall, my brother and I win more than Dad does. We like to tease him when we win. And Dad's a pretty good sport 'cause when we do win, he tells the relatives about all the money we've made. Even though the football boards aren't large bets, my brother and I won a hundred bucks once.

"Dad bets a lot with the bookie 'cause they hang around the same bar. Mom knows about the bookie, and sometimes she really gets upset with Dad about the gambling. I remember one New Year's Day when we had a house full of company and Mom wanted us to eat dinner at a certain time. Dad said we couldn't eat 'cause the Rose Bowl was playing and he had a fairly large bet on it. Plus, my brother, Grandpa, Dad and I all had numbers on a football board for the game.

"Mom and Dad started fighting about the game and the bets. She said it was crazy to let the food go cold, and he said it was crazy not to watch a game that had so much money riding on it.

"Mom lost that fight, and we watched the game. It was so great cheering for Dad's team; every one of us was wound up. When I think about that, I remember the best time I ever had on New Year's.

"Mom buys lotto tickets when she goes to the grocery store. When she gets home, she always puts the ticket on the fridge. That way, my brother and I can look at the ticket and watch the newspaper to see if we win. Sometimes if we go to the store with her, she lets us pick the numbers. I dream about what I'd do if we did win.

"In school with my friends, when football season is over, we bet basketball games. I've played cards for money, but I'm luckier at picking winning numbers, so that's what I mostly do. I've got a friend who went with her parents on a riverboat gambling trip. She said it was real exciting, and I'm going to try it when I'm eighteen. I'd like to go to the casino too. Some of my older friends have gotten in.

"I'm not like some people, though. I would never be so stupid as to spend all my money gambling. People just have to be smart about it like me and not place dumb bets. Besides, I think I would win more than I lose 'cause I'm pretty lucky. That's what Mom tells me. She even wishes some of my luck would rub off on her when she plays bingo every week. I keep telling her it will."

Rick is clearly enmeshed in the introductory stage of gambling. He comes from a family that gambles regularly; his friends all gamble. His father also abuses alcohol. Because of his father's disability, Rick has had to be responsible at a young age, taking odd jobs to earn extra money for the family. He is smart, full of fanciful thinking about his luck, and eager to get on to more exciting forms of gambling.

Life is pretty dull in the quiet little town where Rick lives. The best memories he has involve gambling, and he's ready to do more.

To develop a relationship with anybody or anything, there must be availability. As we discussed earlier, in our country nothing is more available right now than gambling. For that reason, adolescents are being caught in the web of gambling problems that can lead to onset of addiction at a rate that wasn't even thought possible in the past.

Traditional thinking held that many years could go by before people began to suffer seriously or "reach bottom" from compulsive gambling. They might walk the fine line between abuse and addiction for five to eight years. This belief may have been valid for adult compulsive gamblers. However, because of their many vulnerabilities, adolescents progress rapidly toward addiction once the relationship to gambling is established.

Some teen gamblers do not even reach adulthood before the effects of addiction are felt. Emotional immaturity, limited access to money, and restricted loan options all cause the teenage gambler to bottom out quickly. In as little as two years, some kids have gone from experimenting with gambling to full-blown addiction.

The phases as outlined by Dr. Custer provide a basis for understanding how gambling can progress from an innocuous form of entertainment to a deadly compulsion. Although the rate of progression may differ from person to person and the amount of money lost vary depending on income and availability, those who gamble compulsively will reach the desperation phase unless intervention takes place.

The Winning Phase

The introductory period of gambling can be compared to sticking your toe in the water. You try it out to see how you like it. Then, too, initial gambling can be like meeting a new person. Sometimes the friendship clicks, and sometimes it doesn't.

When gambling "clicks" for some people, the relationship becomes so strong that it endures despite obstacles and disappointments. The "click" that cements the friendship happens in the winning phase.

The winning phase is an exhilarating time for a gambler. His enthusiasm for gambling is unequaled by anything else he does. Just thinking about it produces intense flutters of excitement that are matched only by the actual gambling itself.

During the winning phase, the gambler learns the rules and the odds of his particular games of choice. He becomes more skilled at gambling than his friends. He is full of unreasonable optimism about his ability. There seems no reason to pull back from gambling. Why should he? His newfound preoccupation is pleasurable and profitable.

Some recovering gamblers have described the relationship between the gambler and his gambling as almost physical. One gambler describes his experience during the winning phase of the addiction:

"For me, the winning phase of my gambling was almost like starting a wonderful love affair. It was magical, exciting, and I couldn't get enough of it. I thought I had found the love of my life, and from then on everything would be great.

"Gambling was my companion, my date, and I felt my best when she [gambling] was at my side. Gambling loved me because I was winning so much, or so it seemed to me at the time. I could forget all my worries. Gambling gave me the attention I needed, and it was a feeling that I never wanted to end.

"Gambling in this winning phase was not painful or guilt-ridden or shameful. In fact, it was just the opposite, full of innocence, respectability, and happiness. Any pain I experienced was covered over by excitement and attention. I felt so good when gambling that I saw no harm in it, and I wanted my life to be like that always."

The winning phase for a teenage compulsive gambler may last a few months or, at most, several years. Then an unusually long winning streak or a single big win cements the relationship. The win may not be large by adult standards, but the amount doesn't matter. It's the event of winning that commits the teenager to compulsive gambling almost as one person commits himself to another.

A big win, in the mind of a compulsive gambler,

validates his unreasonable optimism. It tells him that his fantasies about free-flowing cash are a reality. "Yes," he proclaims, "I can be rich. If I did it once, I can do it again. I'll show everyone."

Jaime is seventeen and has been gambling-free for ninety days. Through the help of GA, Jaime is recovering from a gambling addiction. Looking back over the past three years, he can see how his compulsive gambling passed through three distinctive phases. He talks about his winning phase:

"My gambling started out being fun. I can remember the first time I bet. I was twelve years old and bet $5 on the Super Bowl game. I won. The next winning I remember was during a church-sponsored trip to summer camp when I was fifteen. We had a big card game going, which started on the bus ride to camp. The chaperons thought we were playing for nickels and dimes. They told us to keep our playing to a minimum, but there were sixty kids and every single one was gambling.

"I played it smart with my gambling. What the camp kids didn't know was that I had been playing cards for money every weekend. They also didn't know I counted cards when I played. So I kept winning.

"Every night we were at camp we gambled on cards. In four days, we had a total of five hours of sleep. Gradually, we eliminated all the losers. (One kid who was a big loser had to sell his head set and a new pair of jeans to get out of debt.) Finally we had a table of only the top players left. I was one of the four chairs in the final game, and I won the pot. Four hundred dollars!

"At home, Mom asked how I liked church camp. I smiled as I told her she wouldn't believe how much fun I had!"

Jaime had found his first love at fifteen, never knowing its embrace would almost strangle him.

CHAPTER 9

The Losing Phase

T he big win signals the end of the first phase and the beginning of the second phase of a compulsive gambler's career. He now enters the losing phase.

At the start of the losing phase, the gambler's overblown optimism turns into outright bravado about his prowess. When he isn't gambling, he is thinking about how soon he can get back into a game. Remembering the winning experience, he increases the frequency and size of his bets, anticipating a still larger win. Naturally, losses occur, but he dismisses them as temporary bad luck.

Knowing that he has put more of his limited money at stake, he becomes irritable and short-tempered, often lashing out at those closest to him. He draws out his savings and sells personal items such as a sports card collection or a CD player, trying to get money to return to the action and break his losing streak. A sense of urgency takes over his gambling, and he begins to chase, betting more in an attempt to recoup his losses.[26]

The young compulsive gambler now just wants to get even, believing that the next big win is only a bet away. He skips school and lies to his parents about his time away from home. He may quit his job, "knowing" he can make more money at gambling if he can only spend a little more time doing it.

Jaime described his losing phase this way:

"Gambling was so much fun after winning the $400 pot. I started increasing the number of nights that I played cards, seeking out more games with people from other schools. My playing time increased too; I went from two hours to five hours a night. This was my honeymoon with gambling. Walking away from something I enjoyed so much wasn't in my plans.

"Gradually, my gambling style was changing. I couldn't leave the table when I was way ahead. It was like I had to bet more. I was going to parties where the pots were five hundred dollars. One party was during a statewide high school hockey tournament. There were kids from all around the state at our hotel, so one night we put tables together beside the swimming pool. Just to get into the game cost $10, and the pot became enormous in no time. I won a couple of hands and then I was dealt a few bad cards. In half an hour I had lost $200—all the cash I'd brought. After finding some friends from my school, I borrowed a couple of twenties and was back in the game.

"But I came unglued. My bad luck continued. I wasn't paying attention, and I made mistakes counting the cards. Losing made me nervous in front of all these city kids. I was mad that I had dropped so much cash to people I'd never see again. What a geek!

"After returning home, I had to rebuild my rep as a winner. I started gambling seriously every night.

Some days I'd leave school during last hour, call in sick to the restaurant where I worked, and head to a party to gamble. I knew I had been a winner, and I wanted to feel like that again. But my bank account was telling me I was a loser.

"The fact that I drained my savings didn't matter, though. I found games with bigger pots. The rule at these games was no change allowed—if you didn't have green money, you didn't play. I tried betting on football boards too, thinking that maybe I'd break my run of bad luck by switching my game. To have more time to gamble and get back to winning, I quit my job just before they fired me.

"I was spending up to fourteen hours gambling on Saturdays. Mom was nagging me for being away from home so much. Lying, I told her a friend of mine was having a hard time and needed me to be around. Fact is, I was the one having a hard time dealing with losing. At first I had wanted to get back the initial rush I felt when I was on top. But that was changing to wishing I could get back enough money to pay off all the friends I owed."

CHAPTER 10

The Desperation
Phase

Then begins the stage in a compulsive gambler's career called the desperation phase. His gambling accelerates at a frenzied pace. Most of his thoughts during the day, and often long into the black hours of night, are preoccupied with gambling. "How can I get more money?" "Where can I find another game?" "When can I next get away to gamble?" "Who will lend me more money so I can stay in the action?"

Having pawned all possible personal items for gambling money, the compulsive gambler may resort to selling the family's belongings. With legal sources of money drying up, and his gambling getting jammed up, the gambler begins to consider illegal means to obtain money.

If the pressures bear down upon the gambler, he may let the family in on his hidden illness, promising to stop gambling if they'll just give him money to bail him out of his temporary troubles. But giving money to a compulsive gambler to pay his debts is like giving liquor to an alcoholic to sober him up. It doesn't work.

Invariably, the gambler gambles again until he is willing to take responsibility for his behavior. And for now, that is usually the last thing he is willing to do. Instead, denying the severity of his problem, he goes back to gambling. He harbors the sincere belief that just one huge win will solve all his problems. Panic sets in. To get money to gamble, he runs scams at school or drops out, steals from his family or employer, and abandons the friends who will no longer lend him money.

Unlike an adult gambler in the desperation phase, a teenager may not be able to gamble alone. If he is by himself in a casino, he stands out and risks expulsion. And if he's a card bettor, he needs other players. What he does do, however, is increase his kinds of gambling or find new games. His gambling buddies may think he is betting only in their games, whereas in reality he has found a whole new round of games at another high school or on the other side of town.

In a state of desperation, the gambler's erratic behavior alienates those who try to help him. He is losing sleep and skipping meals. Oversensitive to comments from family members, he reacts with rage. He's in a state of full-blown anxiety about the possible cessation of his gambling. Soon his gambling world, like a house of cards, begins to tumble.

At this point, facing both physical and psychological exhaustion, he comes to realize that his only remaining options are suicide, running away, imprisonment, or calling out for help. Jaime chose to call out for help in his desperation stage.

"I knew things were getting out of control because all I could think about was gambling and getting the money to do it. I had never been a liar, but now I lied to my mother and I lied to my friends. I started picking up the loose change left lying around the house. Every dime or quarter was important to grab. I started stealing from my mother's purse. I took small amounts at first, then I ripped off her fives or tens. My mother was going nuts trying to figure out what was making me steal from her. She even took her purse to bed with her to keep it safe during the night.

"Some of my gambling friends were dealing drugs to stay in the action, but I couldn't bring myself to do that. Instead, I sold my rookie card collection of Kirby Puckett for half its value. My Walkman and CD player had already been sold cheap, so I began to harass my sister for baby-sitting money I knew she had. One night I lost some huge bets, and all I could think about was how to get my money back. When I asked my sister again, she refused. Arguing and yelling, I blamed her for my problems. If she would just give me some money this one last time, I promised I would never ask her again. She said no.

"I was so furious that I hauled off and hit her smack in the face. God, I couldn't believe I had done that to my little sister! I ran out of the house feeling like a piece of rotten meat. Man, how could I sink so low? I remember thinking I'd caused Mom and my sister so much grief, maybe I should just quietly end it. I wasn't the same person anymore.

"Before I started gambling, I wouldn't have dreamed of stealing or lying or smacking anybody. I was so ashamed of actually hitting my sister that I didn't think I could face another human being.

"The next morning, Mom gave me two choices: See the school counselor with her or face assault charges. I felt so low that I think I would have said yes to anything. I agreed to go to the counselor with Mom. To show you how sick I was, on the way there I began thinking that now the pressure would be off for a while. That would give me time to figure out my next move to get money.

"What surprised me was, once we were with the counselor, I just broke down crying like a baby. He asked a few questions, and the secret of my gambling life started tumbling out. It was like this huge dam broke, and all the mud came sliding out. I told how I had been gambling full time for the past three months. I was over $5,000 in debt, and people were putting the heat on me for the money.

"I knew I needed help, and finally I was ready to ask for it."

CHAPTER 11

Family, School, and Community Problems

L ike other addicts, a compulsive gambler says and does things he never thought he was capable of. The original reasons he began gambling (escape, entertainment, stress release, stimulation) have long been forgotten. Now he simply struggles day after day to recover some of his losses and regain a thread of dignity, which has been destroyed by his continual losing and lying.

A gambling addiction causes him to act in opposition to his value system. Behaviors that once were normal, such as telling the truth, respecting property, and keeping promises, have disappeared. So have many of the material things he held valuable.

A teenager who becomes addicted to gambling is not only disruptive within his family, though that is where symptoms often show up first. Schools and communities also suffer the consequences of a teen's addiction. Because of the lack of information about the effects of teen gambling, however, school administrators and local law-enforcement agencies may not be aware of the causes behind stolen property and absenteeism.

Signs of Problems in the Family

Because of normal family disagreements during the early adolescent years, the family may initially overlook problems that arise. But sooner or later, the effects of compulsive gambling can no longer be dismissed as symptoms of the developmental process.

1. Frequent late-night phone calls. Placing bets after the family had gone to bed or sneaking out to call from a public phone was how Larry, a sports bettor who used a bookie, had to operate. When he hit the desperation phase, he wouldn't take any calls for fear it was the bookie, whom he owed $4,000.
2. Secrecy. Larry hid betting sheets under his bed; he tore up newspapers he used for gathering track results. When he'd go to the track, he'd lie and say he had been with friends. The friends had been bribed to lie for him in case his parents checked out his story.
3. Missing money. Family rainy-day funds, cookie-jar coins, and pocket or purse change were regular sources of Larry's gambling money. No one could seem to explain the losses.
4. Family violence. Having tapped all the easy resources, Larry intimidated and finally blackened the eyes of his younger brother when he threatened to tell their parents about Larry's gambling.

Signs of Problems at School

The circle of those affected widens as the gambling problem grows. Unless teachers and administrators are aware of the consequences of compulsive gambling, they may not recognize what is causing an increase in vandalism or theft.

1. Tardiness. Jesse often sleeps late and misses first hour after a night of blackjack at the casino. Friday afternoons, along with his friends, Jesse skips last hour to get an early start on the weekend poker game.

2. Truancy. Mike has been picked up three times for being truant while playing pool. That doesn't count the days he's gone to the track for the afternoon races.

3. Stealing. The student commissary has been ripped off; $1,000 dollars is missing from the Year Book fund, and the food drive collection barrel on the second floor has been emptied of its goods. Nobody but Dan, who has been an A student until now, knows what is going on. Dan, however, still has $300 outstanding on a poker game and needs to come up with more cash soon.

4. Scamming. Bill has been selling pirated versions of the latest video releases to other students. Even with his bargain prices, he is making enough to keep himself in a game every night. He isn't the only one running a scam: Some other guys have been running sports boards bets, and they only rarely pay off on a win. By selling to the junior high kids, they can make easy money, since the younger students won't cause a rumble about the losses.

Signs of Community Problems

In a society facing escalating levels of violence, it comes as no surprise that stories of adolescent crime are on the rise. Teenage vandalism, gang activity, and theft may initially seem just another act of antisocial behavior. However, because of the money needed to sustain a gambling addiction, a teen's criminal activity may reveal a gambler in the desperation phase.

1. Terrorist calls. Brad's parents have been receiving anonymous phone calls at all hours of the night. Threats to harm the family have been made if Brad doesn't pay the money he owes for sports betting.
2. Robbery. Jesse and three of his friends took the opportunity of a school holiday to visit the home of a friend who owed them $800 for bailouts they provided during card games. Nobody was home, so they rolled a piano out the patio doors and left it in the street as a warning to pay the debt or else.
3. Assault with a deadly weapon. A Florida high school student who had been acting as a bookie for sporting events was arrested on charges of assault with a deadly weapon. In school he threatened another student with a loaded gun, vowing to kill him unless he paid an outstanding gambling debt.
4. Insurance fraud. In an East Coast suburb, the home of a wealthy family was trashed and robbed of jewels and other valuables while the family vacationed. No signs of forced entry were found. When the insurance company investigated the

claim, the fifteen-year-old son, who was staying with friends, was implicated. He confessed under questioning, saying he had done it to pay large gambling debts. "I don't see what's the big deal," he said. "My parents can afford to replace the stuff."

CHAPTER 12

Is Gambling a Problem in Your Family?

Throughout this book, you have learned about the downside of gambling. You have read the stories of teens around the nation who became caught in the snare called compulsive gambling. For the 2 to 6 percent of the American adolescent population who gamble compulsively, life becomes a tangle of lies, manipulation, and broken promises all springing from the roots of addictive gambling.

Perhaps your gambling isn't the problem. Perhaps you've been thinking, "Yeah, I think that's what's going on with my brother (or parents or relatives), but I'm not certain."

Maybe you are afraid others will think you are crazy if you break the silence about the disease in your family called compulsive gambling. After all, compulsive gambling is called the **hidden illness.**

You don't have to wonder or be silent any longer. Lots of kids have families with gambling problems. These kids feel the effects of someone else's gambling almost as much as if they were gambling compulsively themselves. Addictive gambling, like other addictions, spills over onto other family members, who begin to react to the gambler's behavior in an unhealthy way.

The family sees a person they love doing or saying some pretty weird things, and they try to make sense of the behavior. Before they come to grips with the reality of the illness, they often try to make the crazy seem normal. But, crazy is crazy—even if it is someone you love. The mental process of trying to make sense of something that your gut tells you is senseless is called **rationalizing.**

Rationalizing about addictive behavior never works, but unfortunately, it is usually how a family tries to cope as a gambling addiction overtakes one of its members. For example, the adolescent child of a compulsive gambler feels insecure because of the parent's constant criticism or absences from home. If the teenager has not learned how compulsive gambling changes the personality, he or she might feel like the cause of the parent's unhappiness.

One fourteen-year-old whose parent was compulsively doing pulltab gambling recalled, "Mom was gone every night of the week and left me home alone. Until I found out about her gambling, I thought she just didn't want to be around me. I figured she was disappointed in how I looked and acted."

When a gambling addiction is thriving in a home, everything else and everyone else fade in importance. Relationships between members become unbearably strained. Everyone walks around on tiptoes lest they be

the one to say or do something that opens the floodgates
to a verbal tirade or even physical abuse.

A phone call came to Pastor John's house that made
him sit up in amazement. The sixteen-year-old son of a
parish family was sobbing on the phone.

"Pastor, I'm sorry to call you, but I didn't know what
to do anymore. My mom and dad haven't been home
in two days. They've gone to the new casino in South
Dakota, the one that's just across the state line.

"My sisters and I ate the last of the cereal this
morning, and there's no more bread or milk for
supper tonight. Fact is, there's nothing at all in the
refrigerator, and that's the way it's been for about
a week now. My sisters are crying 'cause they're
hungry, and I don't blame them.

"The folks started playing slots about six months
ago. At first, they were laughing and joking about all
the money they were going to make, so I didn't mind
staying home with the kids a couple of nights a week.
But now, Mom and Dad leave me with the kids
almost every night.

"Lately, nobody's home when we get back from
school. I got to do the chores for the animals and I
got to get the supper. When that's done, I've been
sending the little kids off to bed and trying to do my
homework. Mom and Dad usually come home about
midnight, and they're in one lousy mood if I haven't
cleaned up the kitchen.

"I can hear them fighting when they get out of the
car about all the money they've lost. They scream
and yell at each other for staying so long or playing
the wrong slot machines. I try to pretend I'm asleep

just to keep from having them yell at me if the kids have messed up the house.

"Last week, I asked Mom and Dad to stop going to the casino 'cause they only seem to be losing money, but Mom said the casino owed her. Besides, she was feeling lucky.

"So they were gone Tuesday when we got home from school, and tomorrow is Friday. I got to pay the school lunch money for next week, and I don't have it. I used the penny jar to buy some food today, but that's all gone. The girls are crying, and I just couldn't figure out what to do 'cept call you to see if you could help—just till Mom and Dad get home.

"But, Pastor, please don't tell them I called. They'd probably kill me if they knew."

Pastor John, who retold this story, was shocked that a family in his small rural congregation could be so involved with gambling. At first he could not believe that the couple who sat in his church every Sunday morning would ignore the children they loved for the hollow promises of dollar slot machines. But quickly Pastor John learned about the hidden illness of compulsive gambling that knows no cultural, economic, or religious barrier.

Slowly those who live with a compulsive gambler change, too, as the gambler slips deeper into his addiction. They become resentful of the penny-pinching they have to do when memory tells them there used to be enough money, even for extras. They grow frustrated and angry over the load of additional responsibility they have to shoulder to keep the household running. In turn, the family members begin to take out their frustrations on each other.

If you are a teenager living in a family with a gambling addiction, every morning you wake up in dread of the moment when the fighting will start again. Because you may not be certain that compulsive gambling is the problem, or you think that you would betray your parents if you reached out for help, you are engulfed by a feeling of overwhelming powerlessness. Depression sets in, and you find it an effort to get to school or even to get out of bed.

You need help for yourself. You need to get answers for the questions that have been haunting you. You need to reach out to make some sane judgments about the insane situation in which you find yourself. You can get the help you need in several ways.

An organization called Gam-Anon was formed by family members and close friends affected by someone's gambling problem. Gam-Anon has sponsored the formation of Gam-A-Teen groups specifically for teenagers living in a home disrupted by gambling.

The following checklist is adapted from the Gam-Anon family group questions. If you are living with a compulsive gambler, you will answer yes to at least six questions.

Are You Living with a Compulsive Gambler?

1. Do bill collectors constantly call your home?
2. Is the person in question often away from home for long, unexplained periods of time?
3. Does this person ever miss work because of gambling?
4. Do you think that this person cannot be trusted with money?
5. Does this person always promise to stop gam-

bling; then plead for another chance, only to gamble again and again?

6. Does this person ever gamble longer than he or she intended to, until all money is gone?

7. Does this person immediately return to gambling to try to recover losses, or to win more?

8. Does this person gamble to get money to solve financial problems or expect gambling to bring the family wealth?

9. Does this person borrow money to gamble with or to pay gambling debts?

10. Has this person's reputation suffered because of gambling?

11. Has this person ever done anything illegal to finance gambling?

12. Have you hidden money for living expenses, knowing that you and the rest of the family might go without food or clothing if you do not?

13. Do you search this person's clothing, wallet, or purse looking for evidence of gambling such as betting slips, scratch tabs, lottery tickets?

14. Do you hide his or her money to keep it from being gambled away?

15. Have you noticed a personality change in this person?

16. Does the person consistently lie to cover up or deny gambling activities?

17. Do you attempt to anticipate this person's moods or try to control his or her life?

18. Do you find yourself doublechecking this person's stories to verify his or her activities?

19. Does this person use guilt trips or manipulation as a way of shifting responsibility for gambling onto you?

20. Does this person ever suffer from remorse or depression because of gambling, sometimes to the point of mentioning suicide?
21. Has the gambling ever brought you to the point of thinking you should leave or take the family away from your home?
22. Do you feel as if life with the gambler is a bad dream?

If you have thought carefully and answered yes to six or more questions, you have taken a step toward understanding what has been making life in your home seem like an emotional nightmare.

Take another step. Look in the white or yellow pages of the telephone directory or call the Gam-Anon International Service Office—(718) 352–1671—to request free information about living with a compulsive gambler.

Then reach out to a trusted adult friend, teacher, or school counselor. Go to the student assistance program. They can help you find ways of coping with the daily stress that is an inevitable part of living with a compulsive gambler. They will reassure you that you are not alone in your search for a more serene way of life, and they can support you in finding a way to achieve it.

Sarah, the daughter of a compulsive gambler, thought she was all alone in her struggle to cope with a mother who had a gambling addiction. A shy young woman, Sarah decided to share her story because, more than anything else, she wants all you teenagers who are children of addicted gamblers to know that you are not the cause of all the crazy stuff going on. The gambling addiction is not your fault, and you can reach out to others.

"My mother used to have a drinking problem, but supposedly she had stopped. When I was fourteen,

Mom started going out a lot. At first it was just on weekends, but pretty soon she was gone every night. I assumed she had started drinking again, because she smelled like a smoky bar when she came home.

"I was used to being alone sometimes, because my parents had divorced when I was younger. But this was getting ridiculous. I began to wish that just once Mom and her friend would stay with me at night. It got to the point where it seemed like I was the mother and she was the kid. I remember one fight when I screamed, 'You're always going somewhere. Why can't you stay home just one night?'

"We were continually short of money, which really confused me. Mom had a very good job, but overdue bills were stuffing the mailbox. When I asked for money for clothes or school supplies, Mom nagged me about spending every cent she made. This frustrated and infuriated me. How could she complain about my needing money when she was going out every night?

"It wasn't too long before Mom got behind on the rent. Our landlady lived in the same building and started bugging Mom to pay up or get out. So Mom found a cheap little basement apartment, and we moved in. She never told the landlady we were leaving, so I had to sneak back after dark to get our belongings. I felt so stupid crawling through a window into the apartment to pick up my stuff. The whole thing was like a scene from a movie, totally unreal.

"I hated the new apartment. It was dark, and it was miles away from my school and my friends. Not only was I alone every night in this dreary place, but the phone had been cut off for nonpayment. I didn't really mind the distance from my friends, because I didn't want them to see where I was living. But having no phone was really depressing. Now I had nobody to talk to at night when Mom was gone.

"So I sat alone in the dark and watched this tiny television and hugged my cat. I think I would have gone totally crazy without my cat to talk to. I kept thinking I was too young as a seventh grader to be taking care of myself. I knew my friends' families functioned differently, but I couldn't tell them what was going on because I didn't even know myself.

"Gradually, I got more and more depressed, and it showed in my schoolwork. I had been a good student, and all of a sudden my teachers wanted to know why my grades were dropping. I was too ashamed to tell my favorite teacher, Ms. Becker, what was going on with Mom. How could she possibly understand what it was like living in my crazy home? I thought my life couldn't possibly be normal, but because I didn't have anything to compare it to, I didn't know for certain.

"Finally, Ms. Becker had a meeting with Mom. She questioned Mom about my grades and attitude, trying to find out what would cause me suddenly to lose interest in school. I think that was the trigger for Mom to take a look at what her addiction was doing to both of us.

"Not long after that Mom hit bottom, realizing that she had totally lost control of her life to gambling. She came to me and told me that she hadn't gone back to drinking, that she was addicted to pulltab gambling.

"Of course I was relieved she hadn't been drinking, but I was baffled how gambling could be an addiction. Then Mom started going to Gamblers Anonymous. She told me how, once addicted, a person is controlled by the irresistible urge to gamble. The compulsion causes the gambler to destroy just about every area of life, including loved ones. That part she didn't have to tell me; I already knew.

"Mom has been gambling-free for two years now, with the help of GA. I got into in a Gam-A-Teen program, which has helped me deal with my anger and shame about Mom's gambling. I've also learned a lot about myself and how I deal with problems. Knowing that I would rather escape problems than face them head-on has helped me make a conscious decision not to use gambling for entertainment. I'm just too susceptible to using addictive behaviors rather than working out my problems."

Sarah was fortunate to have a caring teacher who saw problems in her students' lives and was willing to reach out and help Sarah. You don't have to wait for someone to notice that you are having problems if there is a compulsive gambler in your life. During your adolescent years, you are learning many ways of taking care of yourself. Asking for help when you need it is one very important part of good self-care that will enable you to become a successful adult.

If you attend a Gam-Anon or Gam-A-Teen program there is no guarantee that the compulsive gambler will stop gambling. But you will find the encouragement, understanding, and support to deal with some of the pain you experience from living in a family where someone has a gambling problem.

CHAPTER 13

Reach Out to

Recovery

The downward slide toward the desperation phase of gambling does not have to happen to all compulsive gamblers. If you are a teenage compulsive gambler, you can find help for your problem no matter what stage of the illness you are in. Some kids are so scared by what they see happening in their life that they ask for help early in the progression.

Others, with less knowledge about addiction and its effects, have to reach bottom before resigning themselves to the fact that their life is on a collision course with disaster. Legal problems, development of a second addiction, or even a suicide attempt may bring them into contact with professionals who can assist them.

Recovery from the illness of compulsive gambling begins the moment you ask for help. Here is how one recovering gambler put it:

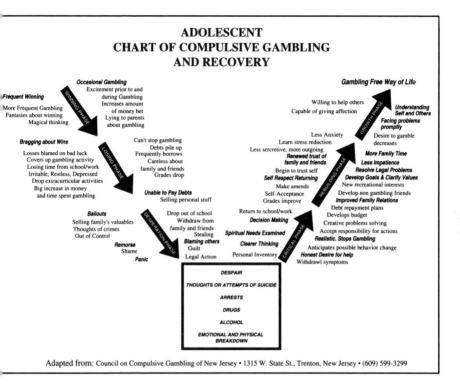

ADOLESCENT
CHART OF COMPULSIVE GAMBLING
AND RECOVERY

Adapted from: Council on Compulsive Gambling of New Jersey • 1315 W. State St., Trenton, New Jersey • (609) 599-3299

"I had lost all control of my life to gambling. Gambling took from me all the things I loved most. Only when I admitted I was beaten and powerless over this illness did I start to gain control of my life again.

"At the end of my gambling, I was so lonely and down that I went to a counselor for my depression. He told me about Gamblers Anonymous. When I went to my first GA meeting, I didn't feel so alone anymore. I found people there who had been where I was. Just seeing people who had gone through many of the same things that I did gave me hope, and I started to feel better from day one.

"When I woke up the day after that first GA meeting, I didn't have to deal with having lost money the night before, and I slowly realized that I didn't have to be a loser anymore.

"As the weeks went by, I made an honest attempt to live the 12-Step recovery program of GA. I continued to see my counselor, and I started accepting responsibility for my past behavior. I began dealing more honestly with those around me. That became easier and easier, because once I stopped gambling I had no reason to lie or manipulate people.

"I made a realistic plan to pay back my debts and tried to make amends for the way I had treated people. Then a funny thing happened. I started to get back some of the important things I had lost— like my friends and my family and my self-esteem.

"The better I felt about what I was doing, the more I enjoyed life. I started to go out again and spend time on some of my former hobbies. But I had one fear. Because I was a sports bettor, I wondered if I could ever enjoy watching games again. To my amazement, I discovered that a football game can be more fun when my stomach isn't cramped up with worry about losing hundreds of dollars!

"When I was gambling, I used to panic thinking about what I would lose if I stopped. The truth is, I was losing everything by gambling. Now I have everything to gain.

"My recovery hasn't been easy, but it has been rewarding. I live one day at a time, knowing that I can choose to gamble or not. Being gambling-free doesn't guarantee a happy life. But by choosing not to gamble today, I know that at the very least I have a life worth living."

Sources of Information and Help

Whatever stage you may find yourself in, believe that help can be yours by talking with a trusted teacher, a school assistance program counselor, or a substance abuse counselor. You can get more information about the illness of compulsive gambling by getting in touch with any of the following:

- Local chapters of Gamblers Anonymous (GA), Gam-Anon, or Gam-A-Teen
- The National Council on Compulsive Gambling
- Where available, a state chapter of the Council on Problem Gambling
- The local community addictions clinic, hospital chemical dependency unit, or adolescent addiction program
- Your state department of health
- A community mental health facility

Additional information can be obtained by calling or writing these resources directly:

Gamblers Anonymous International Service Office, Inc.
P.O. Box 17173
Los Angeles, CA 90017
(213) 386-8789
(Assistance for the compulsive gambler)

Gam-Anon International Service Office, Inc.
P.O. Box 157
Whitestone, NY 11357
(718) 352-1671
(Assistance for the compulsive gambler's family)

Gam-A-Teen
P.O. Box 157
Whitestone, NY 11357
(718) 253-1671
(Assistance for the teenager of a compulsive gambler)

National Council on Problem Gambling
445 West 59th Street
New York, NY 10019
(212) 765-3833 or 1-800-522-4700

Canadian Foundation on Compulsive Gambling
505 Consumers Road
Willowdale, Ontario M2J4V8
(416) 499–9800 or (416) 222-7477

National Center for Pathological Gambling, Inc.
924-26 East Baltimore Street
Baltimore, MD 21202
(301) 332-1111 or 1-800-332-0402

CHAPTER 14

Questions Teens Frequently Ask

Q: Do I have to gamble every day to have a problem with gambling?

A: No. Some people may gamble only once a week or once a month and have a gambling problem. You have to look at the outcome, the consequences of your gambling.

If you seldom gamble, but you lose all your money and steal to replace it, you've got a problem. If you miss school because you were out late at the casino, and you lie to your parents about where you were, your gambling is a problem.

Q: If I think my friend has a problem with gambling, how do I get him to stop without making him mad at me?

A: First of all, keep in mind that if someone you care for is having problems with gambling, the problems are his, not yours. Though it is natural to want to help someone you care about, the person must ultimately be responsible.

Though you can't make someone stop addicted behavior, it certainly is okay to tell him you are concerned. Be sure to use facts based upon what you are really seeing. (Check out the questions again in Chapter 12.) Blaming and shaming should have no part in telling someone how worried you are about his behavior.

Straight talk, backed up by the message that you care, is the way to show your concern.

Q: I confronted my friend about his gambling, but he still doesn't think he has a problem. What more can I do?

A: Nothing! On the surface, that may seem like a heartless and cruel answer. It's pretty hard to stand by and watch someone make all kinds of problems for himself without wanting to step in and take control.

However, if you have let him know why you are concerned and that you are available to be supportive if he decides to get help, you need to let go. In the treatment of addictions, this is called **detaching with love**.

To detach with love, you do not desert the person. In fact, you have pledged support and help when he is ready to get assistance. But for your life not to become entangled with an addiction, you've got to be ready to back away for now.

You might say something like, "Brian, I really care for you, and we've talked about your gambling before. I feel frustrated and angry when you lose all your money and then beg me for more. You're one of my best friends, but I can't be around you when you're gambling. If you decide to quit, I'll be there for you. Until then, I've got to go."

That is a tough stance to take, one that requires you to be strong. But once you've expressed your care and concern, it is time to detach.

Q: I've got to talk to someone. My friends are losing $200 to $300 at school in a floating poker game. No way can they afford it! They started out with lunch money, but now the pressure is on for big pots. What can I do? I don't want to snitch.

A: Your plea sounds as if you're really concerned, and your worry about talking with anyone outside the circle shows how loyal you are to your friends.

Ask to speak with your school counselor in confidence. By asking for help in dealing with your feelings about the gambling going on in your school, you're not snitching. You're taking care of yourself.

Most schools prohibit gambling on school grounds and make the consequences for doing so pretty clear. Your friends can expect some consequences for their gambling sooner or later. It is the administration's responsibility to intervene, not yours. Taking care of yourself and your feelings about the gambling does not violate any rules, but your friends' gambling does.

Q: My brother gambles, and when he can't pay his bookie, he borrows money from me. He tells me he'll get beaten up if he doesn't pay. Is it okay for me to give him money? I sure don't want him to get in trouble.

A: Your brother may already be in trouble and need help. If he is a compulsive gambler, continuing to lend him money is a bailout. It is like giving drugs to a drug addict, or liquor to the alcoholic. It simply doesn't work, but actually prolongs the addiction.

You need help yourself to get out of being intimidated by your brother's pleas. An organization called Gam-Anon has been very helpful in assisting family members of gamblers. Its fellowship teaches how to detach from the gambling, stop bailing out the gambler, and protect yourself from further financial exploitation.

Q: If I'm not eighteen and I win the lottery—or win big in a casino—can I collect?

A: No, you cannot collect unless you are of legal age to gamble, which in most states is eighteen for the lottery and between eighteen and twenty-one for casino gambling.

Q: Can I be too young to be a compulsive gambler?

A: There is no age limit on addictions. Popular belief twenty-five years ago was that no one under fifteen could possibly be an alcoholic. Now there are children in treatment as young as age nine.

Five years ago, only adults were considered compulsive gamblers. Today, we know, fourteen- and fifteen-year-old kids are in serious trouble, and some as young as twelve are heading for trouble.

Q: At graduation, we have a casino night. It was started to help prevent kids from drinking and driving. The casino night, or dry night, has been an alternative to drug and alcohol use as a means of celebrating. Why do they seem to be promoting gambling now if it can be addictive too?

A: That's a good question. Thirty years ago, no one

thought adolescents could be alcoholics. Now we know better. Schools and parents work to educate and prevent teenage drinking. They know that partying with alcohol can have dangerous, even life-threatening results.

The same could be true of gambling. Few people today consider the possibility that adolescents can be hooked on gambling. Most people see gambling as a harmless form of entertainment, which it can be. But with what is known now, a second look should be given to "Las Vegas nights" in high schools.

Perhaps through your Student Council or the PTA, you can help educate others. With information from the National Council on Problem Gambling, you can help them decide whether they want to have a casino night or how they might structure it differently.

Q: If I have a gambling problem, can I still gamble if I learn to control it?

A: We believe that like other addictions, once you are addicted you cannot try controlled usage. A recovering compulsive gambler who experiments with gambling again is like a fireman putting out smoldering embers with a stream of gasoline. At any moment, the whole thing will ignite again.

Glossary

action (1) Term used by gamblers for the thrill, rush, excitement, and enjoyment of gambling. When gambling, the gambler is said to be "in action." (2) Also used by gamblers to describe betting; e.g., "I'm looking for some action," or, "Do you have any action on the game?"

bailout Money given to a gambler to ease financial pressure or pay his debts. By relieving his responsibility, a bailout almost assures that the gambler will continue gambling.

bingo Game of chance in which players cover randomly called numbers printed on a pattern of numbered squares. Computerized play buttons now are used in many high-stakes bingo games.

bookie Person who accepts bets and handles payout of winners for a fee.

chasing Gambler's desire to get even or recoup losses through more gambling. The greater the losses, the more intense the chase.

flipping Game of skill, often involving betting, played with baseball cards or money. The object is flipped off the thumb onto a wall or hand.

handle Total money wagered by all bettors on a game or race.

hot Describing someone winning with unusual skill or luck.

house Business or establishment that sponsors gambling

activities and receives the profits. With lotteries, the state is considered the house.

hunch Inner feeling regarding luck on a game or bet. To play a hunch is to bet money on that feeling.

jackpot The top prize or highest stakes in various games of chance.

jammed up Situation in which gambler has experienced heavy losses and wishes to gamble more (or pay debts) but cannot legally obtain the money to do so.

keno Numbers game played on paper or video. Player chooses randomly selected numbers out of a field of up to 80. Winnings are based on correct numbers chosen.

lottery Contest in which players purchase tickets with randomly printed numbers. Numbers are revealed through scratching ink off or pulling open the tickets.

penny-ante poker Low-stakes card game.

point spread Number of points assigned to a team to even out the differences among the teams.

pulltabs Form of paper slots in which a tab is pulled open to reveal results.

scamming Operating an illegal or unscrupulous business deal or gambling game.

stakes Money or property risked in a wager or gambling game.

system Plan devised by a gambler in an attempt to achieve increased winnings.

video slots Electronic or computerized gambling game like the original mechanical slot machine but using a video display format.

vigorish Bookmaker's handling fee for taking bets, usually 10 to 20 percent of wager placed by bettor.

Notes

1. Jacobs, Durand F., Ph.D. "Illegal and Undocumented: A Review of Teenage Gambling in America." In H.J. Shaffer, S.A. Stein, B. Gambino, and T.N. Cummings (eds), *Compulsive Gambling: Theory, Research and Practice.* Toronto: Lexington Books, 1989.
2. *Commission on the Review of National Policy Toward Gambling.* Washington, DC: U.S. Government Printing Office, 1976.
3. *USA TODAY*, Sports, June 25, 1991.
4. Griffiths, Mark D. "Gambling in Children and Adolescents." *Journal of Gambling Behavior*, Vol. 5 (1) (1989).
5. Lesieur, Henry, Ph.D., and Klein, Robert. "Pathological Gambling Among High School Students." *Addictive Behaviors*, Vol 12, pp. 129–135.
6. Lesieur, Henry. Ph.D., and Heineman, Mary, M.S.W. "Pathological Gambling Among Youthful Multiple Substance Abusers in a Therapeutic Community." In Eadington, W.R., ed., *Gambling Research: Proceedings of the Seventh International Conference on Gambling and Risk Taking.* Reno: University of Nevada, 1988.
7. Winters, Ken, Ph.D., Stinchfield, Randy, Ph.D., and Fulkerson, Jayne, M.A. "Adolescent Survey of Gambling Behavior in Minnesota: A Benchmark." St. Paul: Department of Human Services, Mental Health Division, 1990.
8. Jacobs, p. 252.
9. Jacobs, p. 259.
10. Jacobs, p. 250.
11. Custer, Robert, M.D., and Milt, Harry. *When Luck Runs Out.* New York: Facts on File Publications, 1985.

12. Custer, p. 185.
13. Volberg, Rachel, Ph.D., and Steadman, Henry, Ph.D. "Refining Prevalence Estimates of Pathological Gambling." *American Journal of Psychiatry*, 1988, p. 146.
14. Lesieur, Henry, Ph.D., and Blume, Sheila, M.D. "When Lady Luck Loses: Women and Compulsive Gambling." In *Feminist Perspectives on Treating Addictions*. New York: Springer Publishing, 1991.
15. McEvoy, Alan, Ph.D. *School Intervention Report*, Vol. 4, No. 5. April–May 1991.
16. Winters, Stinchfield, and Fulkerson.
17. Lesieur and Klein.
18. Frank, Michael, Ph.D. "Youth, Alcohol and Casino Gambling." *Recovery Now*, August, 1988, pp. 54, 55.
19. Lesieur and Heineman.
20. Lesieur, Henry, Ph.D., Blume, Sheila, M.D., and Zoppa, Richard, M.D. "Alcoholism, Drug Abuse, and Gambling." *Alcoholism: Clinical And Experimental Research.* Vol. 10 (1986), pp. 33–38.
21. Richard McCormick, Angel Russo, Luis Ramirez, and Julian Taber. "Affective Disorders Among Pathological Gamblers Seeking Treatment." *American Journal of Psychiatry*, Vol. 141 (1984), pp. 215–218.
22. Lesieur and Klein.
23. Jacobs, D.F., Ph.D., "A General Theory of Addictions." In Shaffer, Stein, Gambino, and Cummings.
24. Nakken, Craig, *The Addictive Personality*. Center City, MN: Hazelden Press, 1988.
25. Marston, Albert, Ph.D., Jacobs, Durand, Ph.D., Singer, Robert, Ph.D., Widaman, Keith, Ph.D., and Little, Todd. "Adolescents Who Apparently Are Invulnerable to Drug, Alcohol and Nicotine Use." *Adolescence*, Vol. XXIII (1988), No. 19, Fall.
26. Lesieur, Henry R. *The Chase. Career of the Compulsive Gambler*. Cambridge, MA: Schenkman Publishing Company, Inc., 1984.

For Further Reading

The following information sheets are available at no cost from
Gam-Anon International Service Office, Inc., P.O. Box
157, Whitestone, NY 11357.
"Are You Living with a Compulsive Gambler?"
"Did You Grow Up with a Compulsive Gambler?"
Also available for a minimal charge:
"Living With the Gambling Problem"
"Merry-Go-Round Named Denial"

An information packet is available at no cost from Gamblers
Anonymous International Service Office, P.O. Box 17173,
Los Angeles, CA 90017. Materials included are:
"Gamblers Anonymous Twenty Questions"
"Young Gamblers in Recovery"

Four booklets are available at minimal cost from Hazelden
Education Materials, Pleasant Valley Road, Box 176,
Center City, MN 55012-0176:
"Understanding Compulsive Gambling"
"Releasing Guilt"
"Sharing Recovery, Overcoming Roadblocks"
"Standing Up to Fear"

Suggested reading on self-esteem and self-worth from
Deaconess Press:
What's Wrong with Me? Lonny Owen.
Little By Little, the Pieces Add Up. Stephen Glick.

Suggested reading on self-esteem and self-worth from Hazelden
   Press:
   Feed Your Head, Some Excellent Stuff on Being Yourself.
   Earl Hipp.
   Inside Out. Gretchen Van Kleef Douthit.

Index